What You Don't Know Will Make a Whole New World

What You Don't Know Will Make a Whole New World

A Memoir

Dorothy Lazard

HEYDAY
Berkeley, California

Library of Congress Cataloging-in-Publication Data is available.

Cover Art: Dorothy Lazard (left), Amir Aziz / *The Oaklandside* (right)
Cover Design: theBookDesigners
Interior Design/Typesetting: THE COSMIC LION

Published by Heyday
P.O. Box 9145, Berkeley, California 94709
(510) 549-3564
heydaybooks.com

Printed in East Peoria, Illinois, by Versa Press, Inc.

10 9 8 7 6 5 4 3 2 1

For my parents, Jack and Lavurn Lazard,
who set all that I am in motion.

Contents

one

THE ROAD WEST, 1968

M y family arrived in California the winter after the Summer of Love. Ours was not the journey of eager anticipation of the nineteenth-century gold miners who rushed to the Sierra or of the anxious desperation of the Dust Bowl refugees who came before us. We were reluctant migrants. But all children are. And the three of us in the backseat of that white Pontiac *were* indeed children—my mother, my big brother Albert, and me. My grandmother Ella Baskin had come to claim us. We were the part of her family who had been living, precariously but sometimes contentedly, in St. Louis, away from her and the rest of my mother's clan. This, our first cross-country trip, marked the end of our independence as a nuclear family. The journey along Route 66 was the end and the beginning of everything we had known and would know.

As we traveled long and desolate stretches of highway, with my mother's younger brother Shelby driving, I tried to imagine what California would be like. The nuns at St. Vincent's had told me about the Golden Gate Bridge, which, with my eight-and-a-half-year-old imagination, I thought would be truly golden. We were headed to San Francisco, to my grandmother's house, where we would live. For how long, the nuns at St. Vincent's didn't say.

Uncle Shelby, or "Shirley," as my grandmother called him, was jovial and gregarious. He told us about all the cousins we didn't know we had and the aunts and another uncle we would soon meet. He was an enthusiastic hugger, which I wasn't used to but liked just the same. He was solicitous to my mother and, like her, smoked cigarettes like they were going out of style, so I figured they must be related.

In that car I began to see my mother with fresh eyes. MaDear was not just my mother, our mother, my father's wife. She was part of something larger, more complex than our nuclear family. Her name was Lavurn, but this uncle called her "Sis," which gave me the first hints of her having a role other than mother and wife. She had a family that she had been born into, a mother from whose body she sprang. A father who had already lived and died by the time our journey began. Still, I never felt in those first few days with our grandmother that MaDear and her mother were close. They didn't talk much during our journey. I couldn't imagine them taking long walks together or playing marbles or Chinese checkers or scrubbing each other's backs during bath time like MaDear and I did. No harsh words were exchanged between them, but I sensed that they were strangers, not on the same team. There was an unspoken tension.

I couldn't remember my mother ever having talked to us about her mother. When our grandmother appeared at St. Vincent's Day Home to retrieve us, she could have been the president of Jamaica for all I knew. I had never heard a story about her or seen a picture of her. It wasn't until my brother pushed me toward the Pontiac and I saw our mother in the backseat that I began to think my grandmother could be telling the nuns the truth. And besides, they wouldn't release us to just anybody. Would they?

After a few days of visiting with our father, who had moved in with our oldest half-sister, Mary, we left St. Louis and traveled west along Route 66 and hummed the classic Nat King Cole tune to bide the time. We survived both the curses of racists in Amarillo, who chased us off the sidewalks, and the hellish heat of the Southwest desert. That journey west was the longest time I had ever spent in a car. We didn't break our cross-country trek with a sleepover anywhere, just kept driving and riding after water breaks and pee breaks and food where we could get it.

We made our first stop in Needles, California, just over the state line. Needles. I thought, What a funny name for a place. Were there needles on the ground? Is this where needles were made? Did a lot of seamstresses live there? I didn't know what to expect from the Golden State. It was beautiful in completely alien ways. It was early March and there was no snow on the ground. It wasn't even cold. The landscape was flat as a pancake and vast, dotted with desert scrub. Then suddenly, out of nowhere, we'd see mountains in the distance, so big and majestic they looked like something out of a cowboy movie—decidedly not urban, which was the only environment I knew. The red-brick buildings of St. Louis were nowhere to be found. It was during this trip that I first considered the sky as a separate and beautiful thing distinct from the earth, not just the incidental wallpaper to some cityscape. Out West you could see so much of everything all at once. I sensed California could be something quite literally marvelous. It was wide-open spaces, orchards, ranches, and rolling hills covered in wildflowers like I'd never seen.

The two or three days we spent in that car felt like weeks, but finally, in the second week of March 1968, we arrived in San Francisco at the white two-story duplex at 1139 Cole Street that my grandmother called home. My Uncle Melvin, who lived downstairs with his wife, Beverly, and son, Melvin Jr., greeted us warmly. He was also gregarious, a big guy, taller than Uncle Shirley, with a booming voice and a smile that shone from his mahogany face. The whole Baskin clan, it seemed, was upstairs to meet us. There were "cousins by the dozens." I didn't try to remember all their names as each filed in front of us. There were little cousins, my age and younger, and teenaged cousins, Albert's age and slightly older.

"Say hi," they were told as they trickled in that first night. "These are your cousins from St. Louis."

I looked around the room, shy with all their eyes on me and still suspicious of this mother-daughter connection. For one thing, I noticed my mother didn't look like her mother or her siblings.

She was honey-colored while the rest of her family was a hearty chocolate brown. They were beautiful in their sameness, but different from the woman who was supposed to be my link to them. MaDear was slender, angular, and, what I considered at the time, tall. My grandmother—Mam'Ella everyone called her—was short and wide-hipped, with very high cheekbones, false teeth, and a large mole on her nose that kept her glasses from sliding down her face.

I stuck close to my mother, looking to her for some sign of how to interact with these new people, and also because I had missed her so much after being apart for more than a year. My cousins stared at us, and I, nervously, stared back. I didn't know how to be around cousins. The only cousins I had known were my mother's cousins in St. Louis, all grown men with whom I had only a passing acquaintance. Would these California cousins be protectors? Tormentors? Friends?

In all the hubbub and chatter and milling around, my mother collapsed, overcome by a seizure.

"What's wrong with her?!" some of them asked. The little ones shrieked with fear. Some left the room at the sight of MaDear writhing on the floor.

Everyone froze. Even Albert and I froze momentarily. Having not seen our mother overtaken by a seizure in over a year, and having it happen in such unfamiliar surroundings, we were incapacitated. Self-conscious. Exposed. When we did move toward her to perform the duties we had been so accustomed to performing, we were pushed aside as if we couldn't take care of her. Had we surrendered that responsibility by coming here? Who were we if not her caretakers?

My grandmother got a towel and held it to my mother's foaming mouth while someone else moved chairs and cousins away from her bucking legs.

I realized then how new we were to this place. That lack of familiarity did not sit well with me. Back home in St. Louis we knew where everything was. We knew which men in the neighborhood could lift our mother's dead weight and take her up the stairs to our flat if she was struck by a seizure in the street. We knew where the spoons were that, in those less enlightened times, we would insert into her mouth to "keep her from swallowing her tongue." (There was no regard for her poor teeth.)

Although the afternoon was heading into evening, I was told to go outside. Nervous about being shuttled away from my mother, scared to leave her side, fearing another separation, another seizure, I left the house reluctantly. But how could I resist the chance to go outside on a warm winter night? I couldn't remember the last time I was out on the street at night, and never on a March night without a coat. The shackles of St. Vincent's and St. Louis started falling away that first night in California.

My cousin Donna and her younger sister, Jackie, seven and four years old, respectively, approached me first. They were beautiful girls—nicely dressed, neatly coiffed, with long braids held together by colorful rubber bands. Though younger than me, I would soon learn that they were miles ahead of me in confidence, life experiences, and street knowledge. When I asked Donna about "the Chinese lady" who was in our grandmother's house, Donna patiently explained that Carol was not Chinese but Filipino (a word I had never heard before), and that she was a prostitute (another new word), a friend of the family. Specifically, she was Luke's prostitute. Luke, also upstairs, was an old family friend from back in their days in Chicago. This information just led to more questions, which Donna, rolling her eyes, a little exasperated, kindly answered. We walked to the corner of Grattan Street, with Donna like a junior Junior Chamber of Commerce, telling me about her school and the neighborhood. Her family lived not far away on Shrader Street.

Cousins and aunties and houses pressed together like paper dolls. So many new impressions and images, it all sent my head reeling. At the end of that first San Francisco day, it took no time at all to realize we had landed somewhere that would demand we see ourselves in a different way and respond to new expectations.

Mam'Ella ran a board and care home for foster children. When we arrived in California, she just had one foster child living with her, a teenage boy named Calvin Drake. So Albert had a ready companion, just like he'd had at St. Vincent's Day Home. The two boys would share the front bedroom. My mother and I would share the back bedroom, just off the kitchen. Our grandmother's bedroom was at the center of the house.

My short, sturdily built grandmother was all about business. She was one of the first women I knew who was her own boss. She had business cards printed with a color photo of herself dressed in a white nurse's uniform and cap standing behind an empty wheel-chair in front of the house on Cole Street. A welcoming gesture. The back of the card read:

BASKIN'S NURSING HOME FOR RETARDED CHILDREN
24 hours a Day Attentive Care
10 years and Up

ELLA BASKIN
Owner and Operator

According to my cousins, Mam'Ella had had a series of children move through her home, a recent one being a boy in a wheelchair whom my cousins nicknamed Kevin Corn-on-the-Cob because he liked corn so much. When agitated, though, he would reach into his diaper and smear the walls with corn-speckled feces. Hearing this story, I was more than glad that he was no longer there by the time my family arrived.

Living among extended family was a new challenge. In the context of a larger family, Albert and I had more people to answer to, new rules to learn and abide by. Kids in those days were told to "stay out of grown folks' business," to leave the room when adults were talking. I found this frustrating because so often you were sent out of a room *you* had been in first, and it also made it hard to learn much of anything from the adults. You'd ask a question and get:

"Was anybody talking to you? Chile, stay out of grown folks' business. Go play somewhere." It wasn't like we were overhearing State secrets, but, because of that restriction, our peers became an important, though not always reliable, source of information.

By observing and overhearing conversations from a distance I learned all kinds of things. One of our earliest lessons was that family roles had changed. Instead of MaDear taking care of us, as she had done in St. Louis, Albert and I were expected to take care of her. Her family saw her as an invalid in a way that my brother and I never had. Here in California we prepared light meals for her, kept the percolator going for her endless cups of coffee. Three times a day without fail, we doled out her medicines—Dilantin, phenobarbital, and another pill whose name I've long forgotten. Albert and I lit her cigarettes and ran to the store to buy flints for her cigarette lighter. There was no more watching her move around our kitchen, no more of her homemade peach or blackberry cobblers or steaming pots of chicken and dumplings.

Eating in California, by the way, was another adjustment we had to make. My grandmother was a good Southern cook, but she also ate foods I had never seen or heard of—things like canned tamales that slurped onto the plate like dog food. She accompanied the tamales with Spanish rice, also from a can. This dish made me suspicious of what passed for food in California. My father, a former railroad cook from New Orleans, always cooked rice from scratch. It had been a staple back home in St. Louis, and to find it in a can seemed to violate some basic law of nature. In California we ate a lot of what I thought of as "modern foods," like TV dinners and frozen vegetables. But there were fascinating natural foods to discover in California, too. Coconut, mangos, avocados, and tangerines. Back in St. Louis the most exotic food we had ever consumed was egg foo yung at the Chinese restaurant that our older half-brother Sam would sometimes take us to. But in San Francisco, Chinese food was as common as white bread. Sometimes, when my grandmother wasn't around, MaDear would cook her favorite dish: liver and onions, which we'd eat together (only after she cooked my piece of liver as crisp as a potato chip). After school sometimes I'd peel potatoes and watch her fry up a pan of what she called "osh potatoes" (Irish potatoes) and onions. It reminded me of our home and of her moving around our kitchen with ease and confidence.

Among my mother's younger, able-bodied siblings, I began to wonder why only MaDear was afflicted with epilepsy. MaDear's "fits," as people called them then, distinguished her, and distinguished us as a family. One day I built up the courage to ask Mam'Ella how my mother, her oldest child, came to have such a strange and violent ailment.

Mam'Ella said that someone had "got holt of some of her hair and buried it."

What? I thought I'd misheard her. But I hadn't. She thought it was some kind of curse, like a witch in a storybook would cast. As much as I longed for an explanation for my mother's illness, I could not make myself believe that one. How could the hair on your head have anything to do with what goes on inside your body? But I knew better than to challenge my grandmother. Based on how certain she sounded, I figured this was an old story she had told many times. To press her for an explanation would only get us back to "stay out of grown folks' business." I'd have to find out more some other way.

two

BACK HOME

By the time my parents got together in the early 1950s, they had both been married and had ten children between them. But, to be accurate, by the time I showed up, few of their offspring were still children. My father, whom everyone called Mr. Bear, had been widowed twice. A retiree living on a pension, he was old enough to be my mother's father. MaDear was divorced with three kids, the youngest one a toddler, when she married Mr. Bear. With him she had three more. I was the last in the line. Like most of the Lazard children, I was born at Homer G. Phillips Hospital, St. Louis's segregated hospital. We lived on Franklin Avenue in a cold-water flat over a grocery store. Four rooms plus a toilet shed out on the front porch.

We attended the parish school, St. Nicholas, as our older Lazard siblings had. A devout Catholic, my father dragged us to church every Sunday, ignoring our protests of hunger (in those

My dear mother, Lavurn Lazard, looking elegant in this photo that was taken some years before I was born.

pre–Vatican II days, there was no eating before you took Communion) and our inability to sit still through Mass. Fortunately, St. Nicholas had a "cry room" where squirmy kids could go to ignore the sermons properly. After Mass we'd go home and either MaDear or our father would cook us a hearty breakfast. I'd sit on my father's lap while he read me the comics and my mother listened to music on the radio. And Albert, five and a half years older than me, would head outside to wherever boys went to entertain themselves. After breakfast I could sometimes talk my mother into a game or two of marbles while my father dozed in a chair. I found my mother endlessly fascinating. Sometimes I'd watch her, riveted, as she performed the most mundane tasks: feeding our clothes through the wringer washer, ironing our sheets, or weaving gum wrappers into placemats. I marveled at how busy and creative she was in taking care of us.

I was six or seven years old when MaDear began an extended stay in the hospital. She had been in and out of hospitals all my life, so her stays were never immediately concerning to me. We regularly went to Homer G. Phillips for one thing or another. Albert had been treated for tuberculosis there. We got our immunizations, our check-ups, everything medical there. Sometime in 1966, when our father told us she was in the hospital, I assumed it was at Homer G.

Days went by. Weeks went by. Our father tried to get us to school on time and to church on Sundays. He cooked our meals, but someone and something essential to the

Jack Lazard, my ancient father, whom everyone called Mr. Bear.

family equation was missing. The three of us never got into a cab to visit MaDear in the hospital. Mr. Bear told us repeatedly that she'd be back home soon. My mother's older children, all living in Chicago near their father by this time, were being told the same thing.

If I had to point to one particular thing that changed our fate, and my parents' sovereignty over us, it would have to be my personal grooming. With my mother hospitalized, my hair care fell to my father, who had less-than-wise counsel from Albert. My father was a very old man with very little hair, so his comb was too insubstantial (to put it mildly) to handle my kinks. One day while trying to get me together to head to St. Nicholas, my father got his tiny drugstore comb ensnared in my hair. He tugged. I screamed. Albert intervened, sure he'd know how to get it out. But all the tugging, pulling, screaming, backcombing, and my own vain attempts came to nothing. My old man eventually asked for scissors to free his comb and me from this agony. And off came nearly half my head of hair. One of my torturers redesigned my hairdo in an attempt to make me look less crazy, but the attempt failed.

It wasn't long after this that Albert and I stood in stunned silence in family court while adults we didn't know decided that we should be placed "in care," as folks called it. We were given a choice: I could be sent to live at an all-girls orphanage, St. Francis (where a few of my older half-siblings had been placed many years earlier), or to the coed St. Vincent's Day Home. Albert made the decision that we should stick together. Exactly why we were being sent away or how long we'd have to stay was never made clear to me. No one explained anything to kids in those days. But I figured it had something to do with things that had gone missing: our mother, my braid, and our father's ability to cope with two young kids. Still, that didn't seem justification enough to pull us from the only home we had ever known.

The care was to be provided by nuns at St. Vincent's Day Home in Florissant, a small community between St. Louis and Ferguson,

Missouri. St. Vincent's was a massive three-story brick edifice that was the length of a city block, set far back from North Florissant Road and protected by an iron gate. The residents were segregated by sex and then divided into three age groups each. I was placed in the little girls' room (for girls up to ten years old), and Albert was placed in the middle boys room (for eleven- to fourteen-year-olds). There were no Negro nuns and no Negro lay people. In Albert's age group there were two other Negro boys, the Skinner brothers, to keep him company, but I was not so lucky. So far in the home's fifty-year history, I was the first Negro girl to live at St. Vincent's.

The nun assigned to my room (whose religious name I forgot long ago) introduced me to the other little girls.

"Girls, this is Dorothy Ann. Say hello."

They looked at me as if I was a circus freak—a little bit of terror and a little bit of morbid curiosity. A few gave meek hellos and then went about their business.

The little girls' rooms were bright and sunny, facing the front of the building. There was a dining area with low tables and chairs and a kitchenette that provided just enough space for washing dishes. Beyond that was a play area with dollhouses and baby carriages and plastic tea sets. A half wall separated this area from the TV area, where viewing was strictly monitored and timed. We could watch *Ed Sullivan* on Sundays and *The Monkees* on Monday. Beyond the living room was a large dormitory room. Every four or five beds were separated by big wooden closets with sliding doors, where we kept our few clothes. In the far corner of that room, walled off on two sides, was the nun's bedroom. The walls of our nun's room did not reach up to the ceiling, so she could hear what was going on in the children's sleeping area.

It was still early when the nun announced that it was time to get ready for bed. I had always been a bit of an insomniac, staying up as late as I could to chatter with my parents, play with my brother, or watch TV (though in those days there wasn't much TV to watch at night). The nun led me into the bathroom, where a row of shower stalls lined the far wall. She explained that we girls were expected to shower before bed each night. She handed me a towel and gestured toward one of the free stalls. I looked inside. I had never taken a shower before. In my family we bathed in big galvanized tubs positioned in front of the open stove. My mother would fill the tubs with hot water from the kettle or a big pot, and Albert and I would swish around, happy, until the water got cold.

I wondered what Albert was doing now on the other side of this strange building. Was he being made to go to bed so early? Did he know how a shower worked? Were the boys staring at him as if he had landed from another planet?

I looked at the shower handles, then back at the nun. I didn't need to explain. She reached in and turned on the water, then took my hand and drew it under the flow, checking with me to see if I found the temperature okay. There were no kettles to fill here, no ovens to sit in front of to keep warm. I marveled as water rushed out of the showerhead.

This was the day I got an inkling of how little white people knew about Negroes. When I got out of the shower, my fresh press-and-curl, which our neighborhood beautician had so lovingly given me before I headed off to parts unknown, had reverted back to my natural kinks.

"What do I do with it?" the nun whispered, sounding bewildered as she patted my spongy wet hair.

"You press it," I said.

"Press it. How do I do that?"

I looked at her quizzically. "With a straightening comb," I said. I didn't know how to better explain it. How could she not know this? She was an adult, after all.

"Where do we go to get it back the way it was?"

"On Franklin," I said, figuring that the nun would send me to my old neighborhood to get my hair done, and I wouldn't return. I assured the nun I knew how to get there. I had paid attention to the route they took from our house to St. Vincent's. I could surely retrace it. But she told me that she'd figure out what to do.

I was incredulous. I didn't have the same kind of hair as the other little girls. I didn't know what kind of hair the nun had, or if she had any at all, as her head was fully covered with a wimple. She combed gingerly through my hair, going as slow as molasses. It was clear to me she was trying not to hurt me, but I felt suddenly, and for the first time, ashamed of my hair, which had never made me feel any particular way before. It was just *my* hair, like my mother's hair and my brother's and my neighbors'. But with all those watery blue eyes upon me, with all those confused, disdainful gazes, I sensed I was an alien in foreign territory. They made me feel like a specimen, studying and fretting over me. Albert, I was certain, was having no such problem. Boys had it easy that way.

At one point the nun leaned down and whispered, "My real name is Dorothy, too." She sent a big grin my way, which warmed me. "But don't tell the other girls."

I nodded. I liked having someone trust me with their secrets. It made me feel grown-up, responsible, and worthy. All the best movies were about loyalty, so I made a pact to keep this secret, no matter how small.

At home I had never gone hungry. Mr. Bear had been a cook, after all, and though he was as old as tree bark, he still enjoyed cooking. But at St. Vincent's there was a level of abundance I had never known. Toast, swimming in butter, was delivered to our room each morning in big plastic containers. We didn't have to watch how much sugar we put on our cereal. There was meat at every meal. We had fish on Fridays, just like at home, but in the form of fish sticks instead of the smelly mackerel croquettes my father loved.

Between meals and after school, there were games to play, and when the weather turned foul we had a big gymnasium where we'd play basketball and four square to expend our youthful energy. At bedtime our nun would play Broadway musical soundtrack albums. Being lulled to sleep by Rodgers and Hammerstein and Lerner and Loewe was not a bad way to surrender the day, even in unfamiliar surroundings. Still, I missed listening to the radio—Arthur Godfrey's friendly chatter and big band music and Ray Charles singing "Hit the Road Jack." I missed the unsupervised television diet I had grown up with. At St. Vincent's, there were no more cowboy shows. Goodbye, Rifleman; goodbye, Paladin; goodbye, Little Joe Cartwright. No daytime game shows with Kitty Carlisle. No more watching TV until the Indian head test pattern came on and one of my parents said, "Cut that durn thing off."

St. Vincent's was all about regimens and chores. If they don't do anything else to you, the Catholics will certainly work you to death. We were made to make our beds daily. Hospital corners, please! We had to make sure the areas around our beds were tidy at all times, dust the wooden baseboards in our large dormitory, and wash breakfast, lunch, and dinner dishes. In spring we took big baskets out to the orchard in the rear of the property and picked strawberries, some of which would be made into jams. In fall we picked apples and pears.

I made friends with Debbie and Cecilia, who slept in beds on either side of me. Like me, they were not orphans at all, just girls whose families were having a rough time of it. Knowing this about them alleviated a lot of my fears and shame about being at St. Vincent's. So many of us were simply in a holding pattern until our families could get their acts together.

Some days when it would get too hot outside, the three of us would sneak out of the orchard with a basketful of stolen berries and head to the wooded area beyond the orchard. There, a stone grotto stood in the cool shade of trees. It was close enough to the orchard and the building that we could hear if anyone called us back into service, but it was a wonderful hiding place. In the grotto a white statue of a female saint stood, solemn and angelic. Debbie, Cecilia, and I shared stories about what we'd do if the statue came to life, like Our Lady of Fatima had done for the three children in the movie *The Song of Bernadette*. If we could communicate with this stone saint, what would we ask for? And how quickly could she answer our prayers? I had a single prayer: to be back home.

Older girls at St. Vincent's worked in the laundry, operating big machinery that intrigued me. The starchy smell of freshly pressed sheets was intoxicating. And though I wanted to go home, I would have jumped at the chance to work in the laundry when I was older. One day the latch on a huge pressing machine didn't catch, and the pressing plate fell on a nun's hand. The smell of burning flesh permeated the playground. There was a clamor inside the building, calls for help that drew us closer to the laundry windows. When the ambulance arrived, we were all shuttled away, but we watched from a distance as the injured nun was loaded into an ambulance and taken to the hospital. Another girl told us what had happened: the pressing plate had seared the nun's hand and she couldn't free it. That cleared up any aspiration I had for laundry work.

Occasionally I saw Albert passing in the halls during the school day or outside on the playground. He'd come over sometimes to check on me, and I'd ask when we were going home. He couldn't say. One day he was pushing me on a swing but then stopped to rest on a bench a few feet away. Albert stretched out his arms along the back of the bench and dared me to go higher. I pumped and pumped my legs. When I was as high as my little legs could take me, I saw a tall, ruddy-faced white boy with strawberry-blond hair walk behind the bench Albert was sitting on. He watched me for a moment. Then, without saying anything to either of us, he bent down and wrapped his forearm around Albert's neck and started to strangle him. My brother gasped and clawed at the boy's arm, yanked at his hair, his feet kicking like he was pedaling a bike. He scratched at the boy's pimply face. I screamed, "Stop it!" and leaped from the swing set. I ran over and pelted the boy with kicks and punches. I pulled at the collar of his shirt, tearing at his neck. For a moment he seemed unfazed by my efforts to save my brother. Albert pulled at the boy's ears. Then, just as quickly as the attack had begun, it stopped. The boy simply walked away, breathing heavily but otherwise silent. I don't remember what, if anything, my brother and I said to each other or if we reported it to any of the nuns. I was suddenly afraid for Albert. Here I had been thinking that he had it better, being a boy, not having to deal with hair or dolls or being the only one. He had the Skinner brothers, after all. But boys were violent in a way that girls were not. They played rough and, in a snap, the play could turn into a real fight.

We were marooned there, Albert and I, in this strange world of enshrouded white women and awful white kids who'd come up to you and rub your skin to see if the color could be rubbed off. Some of them even admitted to having never seen a Negro before, something I couldn't imagine. Everywhere I had ever been there were Negroes. I hadn't come to realize that that impulse to hate or kill what is foreign is as ancient as the moon and as universal as heartbeats. Despite this realization, I was glad that my friends Cecilia and Debbie could care less if my hair or skin or background were different from theirs.

What You Don't Know Will Make a Whole New World

We were Negroes back then. It said so on our birth certificates. And it was there at St. Vincent's that I first learned the implications of that word. Prior to our arrival there I was just me—my mother and father's baby, my siblings' kid sister. I was not a race, not a minority. Not a social services statistic or a ward of the state. Just Ann Lazard, what my family called me. And while I certainly knew that there were white people in the world, they had not been much a part of my existence. Sure, there were the priests and nuns at St. Nicholas Church and the parish school, and the white guy who would ever so often come to yank our phone out of the wall when my father failed to pay the bill, and all those white cowboys and game show contestants and old-time crooners like Perry Como on television, but other than that, my world had been predominantly and pleasantly Negro.

This new world we lived in demanded that we see ourselves in a new, discomforting way. It required that we establish for ourselves an armor and an awareness that recognized our twin identities—our individual selves and our public, racialized selves. The selves we make and the ones we're told that we have. I felt this duality, this negotiation, even before I had language to describe it. It would become a source of steady irritation in the coming years as I learned what it required of me.

In April 1967 we were to be confirmed, our nun told us, to become official members of the Catholic Church, vowing to uphold its rules and adhere to its codes of conduct. The nuns offered me a book of saints that included a little biography and colored illustration for each. I was to thumb through this saintly book and select a holy figure to be my spiritual guide for the rest of my life. It seemed all of the saints had been murdered for some minor infraction like praying, telling others to pray, being a woman, seeing a spirit, walking in front of Roman soldiers, living anywhere near Roman soldiers. And while the idea of making or witnessing miracles appealed to me, I couldn't imagine how any of this would have anything to do with my life. When would I ever be in Rome?

But that was the thing about Catholicism, and perhaps about all religions: so much was unexplained, mysterious. Lots of pomp and a whole lot of circumstances. For instance, we were made to go to confession weekly. But what had I done to confess? Nevertheless, the priests wanted a story every week, no matter how benign. So I fed them stories. Even back home when we attended St. Nicholas, where I had made my First Holy Confession the year before, I couldn't think of anything I had done to make a worthy confession. Albert's sins were much more substantial—he was an aspiring kleptomaniac—but I was too afraid to lay claim to them, as they were too advanced, too daring for a girl my age. I instead copped to the vague "having evil thoughts" and to occasionally pushing another kid, or calling someone a "bad name." Thankfully, the priest never pressed me for details, as I would've done in his position. Hardly worth the time spent entering the confession booth, I thought. I was curious about the currency of punishment, though. Did the punishment for a lie equal the punishment for a shove? Did the priest have a scorecard he consulted? The rituals of the Catholic Church left me confounded, with more questions than answers.

I picked Rosa of Lima as my patron saint, a little Peruvian girl with short, dark hair and big, sad eyes, because her face was brown like mine. That was as rational a choice as I could make at seven and a half. (I also had an older half-sister named Rose, whom I wanted to honor in some way.) There I was, having been surrounded by white faces for a couple of months, and now I was about to be indoctrinated into a white church ritual that I didn't understand. Maybe, I thought, brown Rosa could help me understand. Maybe she was also being made to confess "sins" that someone else defined as trespass. This confirmation would be the first decision about my life that I could make on my own. I didn't want to mess it up.

The ceremony took place at a grand cathedral, with the Archbishop of St. Louis officiating. He was old and very slow, and I was stationed near the end of an incredibly long line of girls, all of us dressed in pretty white dresses and scratchy lace-trimmed socks. In those days much of the Mass was in Latin. I didn't know what was going on. I did know that when the archbishop came to me I was to speak Rosa's name and formally accept her as my spiritual guide, and by doing so I would be welcomed into the Catholic faith as a true and willing believer.

But I had to pee. The realization came to me suddenly, and the need was urgent. And the man with the dress and mitre was moving *so* slow! I tried to hold on. I had to hold on! I didn't want to have an accident. I wanted to cry. Maybe letting water leak out one end would keep water from coming out the other end. I looked behind me to see if I could signal the nuns about my distress, but they craned their necks and twirled their fingers, signaling me to turn back around. I wondered if I could jump the line. What fate would befall me if I did? When things got to a critical point, I simply ran out a side door of the church, but I had waited too long. A warm stream coursed down my leg as I reached the courtyard. Our nun came out and guided me to a restroom, where she tried to dry me off with paper towels. Though I was not emotionally invested in the ceremony, I knew that she was, so I apologized to her over and over again. After a few moments, I was put back on the line to get officially confirmed. Humiliation knows no bounds. I returned to St. Vincent's with wet socks and wet patent leather shoes and a freshly minted soul that I hadn't realized needed saving.

three

AN EAGER BEAVER

In San Francisco I was enrolled at Grattan School, conveniently located around the corner from my grandmother's house. Holes in our backyard fence and in the school fence made getting to class on time easy. I was told that I'd be in the "high third grade"—a new concept for me—which was the second semester of third grade. I was delighted to discover that there were all kinds of kids there: white kids, Chinese kids, Filipino kids, Mexican kids, Japanese kids, racially mixed kids, and, best of all, Negro kids like me. Lots of Negro kids. I wouldn't be the fly in the sugar bowl anymore. With such a stew of kids, I didn't know what to expect.

Albert was enrolled at Polytechnic High School on Frederick Street, across from Kezar Stadium. Our five-and-a-half-year age difference finally felt significant. We wouldn't be in the same school anymore. I'd have to rely on my cousins to guide me through this newness.

What You Don't Know Will Make a Whole New World

At recess, kids swarmed Grattan's schoolyard like ants at a picnic, running, jumping, chasing each other. Screaming with glee. I felt free for the first time in over a year, or maybe for the first time ever. No more nuns. No more scheduled recreation. Play was a major activity in our Haight-Ashbury neighborhood. Games of jacks, jump rope, four square, hopscotch, Chinese jump rope (with linked rubber bands instead of twine). Card games like War and Old Maid. Hide-and-seek. Red Rover. And the play only got wilder once we were released from school. Together we raided the candy display at Harry's corner grocery store on Cole and Alma Streets, grabbing Charleston Chews, Chick-O-Sticks, and Jolly Ranchers, tossing our pennies and nickels on the counter as we ran back out into the streets.

I made fast friends with the two girls next door, Stephanie Tisdale (my age and in my class) and her younger sister Hap (whose real name was Amy, but no one ever called her that). They were friends with my cousins Donna and Jackie, who lived a few blocks away on Shrader Street. The girls folded me easily into their circle. Surrounded again by people of my own race was an immediate comfort. Stephanie and I did everything together. We played with her dolls, traded food the other didn't like at lunch, and never let on to Vice Principal Plummer, who monitored the cafeteria during lunch, when we dumped our succotash into our empty milk cartons. We were best buds, for sure.

The only thing besides dinner that could drive us into the house from playing was when someone, usually someone's mother, would yell out the window that some Negro was coming on television. Negroes on TV were rare in those days and a source of pride, gossip, and speculation.

"James Brown on *Ed Sullivan*!"

"The Supremes coming on *The Hollywood Palace*!"

We were so starved for anybody on TV who looked like us that we'd watch any entertainer who managed to breach the show-business racial security gates. Moms Mabley, Louis Armstrong, the Temptations, Sammy Davis Jr., the Four Tops. We didn't care what they were doing—singing, telling jokes, dancing, playing jazz cornet. They were us and represented our possibilities in all their myriad forms. It was in this way that I learned that being Negro had a social currency, valued in one community, undervalued in another.

The world careened at me at full throttle in California. But nothing seemed to have as many hidden implications as one Thursday in April, just a few short weeks after our arrival. I rushed home to watch *Dark Shadows* to find out who vampire Barnabas Collins would be biting. This gothic soap opera cleared our street of children each afternoon. I was at home with my mother, who was sitting in the living room looking out the window at the world she rarely engaged in.

I had been watching the TV for about ten minutes, waiting impatiently for all the chatter to stop and the biting to begin, when the program was interrupted. The local news anchor reported that in Memphis during a garbage workers' strike, Dr. Martin Luther King Jr. had been shot and killed. Above the anchor's shoulder was a photo of Dr. King. I couldn't make any sense of it. Garbage workers, a doctor, Memphis (where was that?), a murder. Then almost immediately, Walter Cronkite, the network newsman, came on the screen, and it was then that I knew I wouldn't ever find out what Barnabas Collins was up to that day.

It seems almost blasphemous to admit now that I didn't know who Dr. King was until the day he died, but that is my reality. He was just a face in a frame on my grandmother's mantel. He could've been one of the many relatives I didn't know. I sat spellbound that afternoon watching the news of the hunt for his killer, the strike he had tried to negotiate, the public shock and unbridled grief. Outside I soon heard ambulances, people crying, panicked voices. I was moving toward the stairs to go outside when my grandmother bounded up the stairs, breathless. Seeing her distressed, I followed her back into the parlor, where MaDear had taken a seat near the television.

Mam'Ella shook her head repeatedly, as if she had been overtaken by a nervous tic. She clutched my hand so I stood still, watching her and the television, trying to make sense of why someone, anyone, would kill a man who was obviously so important to so many people. Tears rolled down Mam'Ella's face as she muttered, "Jesus wept" and "Lord, have mercy," and only released my hand when her face was so drenched with tears she had to find a handkerchief. She didn't wail, but her grief was palpable. Then she said something I would hear her say dozens of times afterward: "I hope it wasn't nobody colored."

My mother just said "uh uh uh," over and over again, her lips pursed in a pained expression.

I didn't share their grief but, seeing it, I did feel an enormous bolt of anxiety sweep through me. I began to understand that we had lost someone valuable I didn't know we had had. By the time the news alert was over, so was *Dark Shadows*. I wandered outside and met Stephanie and Hap, who seemed as bewildered as I was by the news. Soon there was a cluster of kids standing confused on Cole Street.

"We should beat up some white people," someone suggested.

"Like who?"

Hunched shoulders. "I don't know. Anybody we can find."

So we seven-, eight-, and nine-year-olds set out looking for victims, looking for retribution. We walked up one block to Parnassus Street, then down to Carl. No white people who we could do any damage to. Before we got to Frederick Street, a Negro man walking briskly crossed the street and said in a clenched-teeth whisper, "Get home! All of you kids, get home right now!" We didn't know this man, but we didn't question him either. Sensing impending danger, we scattered.

Later that evening, as we watched coverage of the riots erupting all across the country, I came to understand why we were given the warning. Cars set on fire, businesses looted and set ablaze. Police in helmets, chasing people and swinging billy clubs and toting big rifles. The stranger on Cole Street wanted us safe and off the streets, likely fearing that our community would descend into the same kind of violent spasm. Fortunately, there was no such outburst.

What You Don't Know Will Make a Whole New World

A buried memory was loosened that day and popped up in me like a buoy. The last time I watched that much breaking news with this level of public reaction was when I was four and President John F. Kennedy was killed. My father and all the adults cried, and the ambulances wailed, and my older brother and sister came home early from school, and the people outside shouted in disbelief and shock.

We were someplace else but, it seemed to me, back in the same place. And in those days no one told kids what to make of the world outside of our childhood, of the chaos that sprung like a jack-in-the-box when we least expected it. Grown-ups didn't tell us about the racial injustice that prompted the protests, or the violence that tried to stop them. They didn't speak of the daily humiliations they suffered or the injustices that drove them to California in the first place. They just wanted to keep us safe, fed, and happy for as long as they were able.

School was my salvation and my ticket to better understanding the world.

Grattan School was a two-story stucco building that sat wide-hipped and welcoming on Grattan Street. My teacher was a white woman named Mrs. Wyke. After years of being taught by nuns, I found it interesting to have a teacher whose wardrobe changed daily. She was popular with my classmates, so I wanted to impress her by being a good student, figuring if she liked me, they would like me. I had always loved school and was eager to learn anything that could fit into my head. In school I was what the old folks called an "eager beaver."

—————

My hand shot up and I stretched my arm as high as I could. "Ooh, ooh, ooh! I know the answer! I know it! Mrs. Wyke! Mrs. Wyke! I know!"

I was on a roll one day. I knew all the answers, it seemed, and had already answered two previous questions. Answering correctly always gave me an effervescent feeling, like when you drink soda too fast and the bubbles get in your nose. Mrs. Wyke called on another student. Then another. But I kept my hand up just in case she wanted to call on me again.

Mrs. Wyke did finally call on me. She said: "Come with me."

I sprang from my seat and followed her into the cloak room. Maybe she wanted me to help her with a project for the class. The cloak room was where she stocked construction paper, glue, and crayons. I stood near the wall that separated us from the classroom, waiting for instructions. Mrs. Wyke bent down close to my ear as if to whisper something, and then she placed her hand gently on the back of my head before she pushed me sharply toward the wall and the row of coat hooks mounted there.

"You be quiet!" The words slithered icy hard out of her mouth.

I had resisted her shove just enough to keep her from driving my eye into one of the hooks. Instead, the bridge of my nose met the curved metal with force.

"Now, go back to your seat."

I felt dizzy as much from the pain to my face as the shock of a teacher assaulting me. I didn't want to go back to my seat. I wanted to go back to St. Louis! At least there the nuns—who definitely believed in corporal punishment—did not attack me without cause. No one had ever treated me with that level of violence before.

I was silent for the rest of the day.

I don't remember when or how I told my grandmother about what had happened in class, but my Aunt Katie, Donna and Jackie's mother, went around to the school to talk to Mrs. Wyke. Aunt Katie, one of my mother's younger sisters, had four kids attending Grattan. Unlike my mother, she was sturdily built and had a tongue as sharp as a knife. She reported back to us that she had told Mrs. Wyke, in no uncertain terms, that if she ever touched me, or anybody else in the Baskin family, that she'd have her face shoved into a coat hook and more. Wow! I felt protected in a way that I never had before, like I was part of a clan. Katie was someone who could set things right and wasn't afraid to let anyone know it. I had a defender!

Still, I was afraid to return to class. I didn't know if Mrs. Wyke was mean to me because I was new or because I was Negro or because I was smart, or maybe because of all those things, but for the rest of the term, I sat back listless, uncomfortably quiet. I let other kids raise their hands and get the honor of being right. I turned in my homework, got good marks, but, as I nursed my bruised nose, I gave nothing back to Mrs. Wyke. From me she got nothing extra, nothing that would make her think she was special, no "thank you," no smiles at the end of the week, no "please, ma'am," no end-of-the-year handmade "enjoy your summer" card. In a way, I wanted her to come at me again so my brave Aunt Katie could, as she promised, "put a foot up her ass." Still, I longed for my home in St. Louis because I was finding, when I least expected it, California could often be too much to deal with.

four

THE WORLD OUTSIDE MY DOOR

Fourth grade was an altogether different experience. I was no longer the new girl. I had learned the ropes. I had made friends, developed routines, and had some knowledge of my neighborhood. And, best of all, I had a kind and dedicated teacher, Mr. Eckart. He was smart, patient, and good-natured, and he gave us interesting homework. All around the class he had posted maps of different countries of the world and national flags, and I fell in love with their shapes and stories. He taught us about the Spanish explorers who braved long sea voyages to get to California. All

My first California school picture, age nine, fourth grade, Grattan School, San Francisco. (San Francisco Unified School District)

the stories were about white men in funny clothes on white horses looking out into the distance for some land to "discover" somewhere else. Anza, Balboa, Cabrillo, Drake, and Portolá.

Fourth-graders in California were also required to learn about the Catholic priests who created the mission system that abused and decimated the Native American population. But in those days teachers skimmed right over the stories of forced labor, tribal removals, and massacres. As in the movies, the Indians, as we freely called them then, had no starring roles in our textbooks. It was just like the slaves, who had no story to tell and were only mentioned when discussing why we should honor Lincoln for freeing them. Pioneer and Jesuit manifest destiny was a brutal business, but nine-year-olds in California were never told that. We were told it was something that had to be done in order to "civilize the natives" and expand the country. The only Native Californian we learned about was lonely Ishi, the last Yahi, who was brought to Berkeley to be studied like a dinosaur bone. I wondered what had happened to his family, his friends, and his fellow tribesmen. How did the white men who took him to Berkeley know he was the last one? Had they killed all the others?

The only Negro who appeared in our lessons in California history was James Beckwourth, who cleared a path for immigrants to California to reach the cities and towns many believed to be lined with gold. Though I was happy to see him included, I couldn't help but wonder where the other Negroes were. And what became of him? Was he the only Negro in California then, and, if so, what could that have been like for him? Mr. Eckart's lessons about frontiersmen

Mr. Eckart and my wondrously diverse fourth-grade class. (San Francisco Unified School District)

and Gold Rush miners played out in my imagination like those old Joel McCrea and Randolph Scott movies my brother Albert and I used to watch on TV. Every tale, like every TV show, glorified white men. I was just beginning to understand that whoever tells the story gets to be the hero of the story.

Despite the limitations of our textbooks, Mr. Eckart wanted us to appreciate history and respect other people's cultures. In his class we learned that culture was the package that our experiences with our families, neighbors, and friends came in. Culture taught us how to become who we would become. Mr. Eckart had lived in Japan for a time and taught us a few Japanese phrases like "Doko desu eki wa?" I didn't know when I'd ever get a chance to ask anyone

"Where is the train station?" in Japanese, or even if he was saying the sentence correctly, but I was excited to learn something so foreign, and I repeated the phrase like a mantra. One day, as he told us about the importance of the tea ceremony in Japanese culture, he carefully wrapped himself into a kimono, sending the class into giggles. It looked like the crepe de chine robes that my Aunt Beverly (who lived downstairs from us) wore. Another day he took us on a field trip to the Japanese Tea Garden in nearby Golden Gate Park, where I saw my first koi fish and ate my first candy wrapped in edible rice paper, which I thought was the coolest thing.

Through his engaging stories, he encouraged us to become citizens of a world far larger than the one we kids now occupied. The fact that he even thought of us as citizens was inspiring. Mr. Eckart helped me understand that geography was history's twin; you couldn't really appreciate one without knowing the other. I found that I could hold lots of history in my head if I could look at the lessons like a story, like a movie—complete with titles scrolling past. And with maps I developed an understanding that the shapes of countries had something to do with their histories as well.

Inspired by Mr. Eckart, I wandered aimlessly through my Haight-Ashbury neighborhood on my own voyages of discovery, peering into shop windows, watching the streetcars rattle into and out of the N Judah tunnel, buying a pierogi (a hot turnover) from the Polish bakery on Cole and Parnassus whenever I could scrape up the change, looking into the darkness of Maud's, the local "dyke bar." These aimless, solitary walks were my way of reclaiming a part of me that had been put aside while I was at St. Vincent's Day

Home, where all activities were scheduled, monitored, partnered, and timed.

Before our stay at St. Vincent's I had begun to amble farther and farther away from my family home on Franklin Avenue, past St. Nicholas School, and down to the shoe factory and past the Ralston Purina factory. One day I got as far as the rail yards and Union Station, from which I made it downtown to the St. Louis Public Library. On my way home, a cab driver pulled over and asked if I was lost. I told him no, because I most certainly knew my way.

Ignoring my response, he pulled over and said, "Let me drive you home. Someone must be worried about you."

I tried to assure him that I could make it on my own, but he convinced me to hop in. So I did. When we arrived at our flat, my mother was standing outside, looking stricken, her thumbs tucked tightly between her first two fingers, her sign of anxiety. She breathed an audible sigh of relief when I bounded out of the cab excited about the ride. The driver got out, too, explaining that I must have gotten lost. I declared that I was not. Then my mother turned to me and said, "In the house."

In San Francisco, I could wander freely—to my cousins' house on Shrader Street to watch Elvis Presley movies, or to Cole Hardware to prowl the aisles of tools and fixtures, or to little Grattan Playground on Stanyan Street. I just had to be back home by dark or dinner, whichever came first.

San Francisco enticed. There were so many things I had never seen before. I was regularly in a state of wonder, marveling at the ornate Victorian houses that leaned into each other, streets so narrow they barely warranted a crosswalk. And so many new smells—patchouli, cloves, and lots of marijuana. You could have dropped me in Marrakesh and I wouldn't have been any more disoriented than I was those first several months in San Francisco.

Outside! I loved being outside. It was where we kids found out who we were going to be. There were followers and leaders, loners and kiss-ups, popular kids and kids with "cooties." There were friendly kids and, of course, bullies. Childhood, like the streets of a new city, I learned, was territory one learned to navigate. One day you're friends with someone, and the next day, they might not be able to stand you. But being outside, trying to make sense of it all, was the best game in town for kids back then.

Though I was outside a lot, I tried never to stray too far from the house that first year in California. My mother, I was sure, needed me, needed to know that I was nearby. And I needed her, too. Knowing she was relatively well and not in some faraway hospital, enduring who knows what, eased my mind. MaDear rarely ventured outside, so she had no friends to speak of, just her siblings who came over frequently and smoked cigarettes and watched TV with her. She no longer went to church. Occasionally, feeling some compassion for her cloistered existence, we kids—Donna, Jackie, Stephanie, Hap, and I—would bound up the stairs and run through the house, with my mother chasing us, throwing her amber medicine bottles at us when she couldn't catch us, pretending to be bothered by our intrusion. We loved being chased, and she loved seeing us having fun.

One day we kids gathered in Mam'Ella's bedroom, which was

located at the top of the stairs. We sat on the floor, in as true a circle as we could manage while squeezed between the bed and the dresser. Someone had brought a Ouija board and suggested that we hold a seance to bring back Emmett Till and Martin Luther King Jr. We were in the midst of our incantation, our eyes closed, deep in concentration and psychic will, when one of the three doors to the bedroom squeaked open.

We screamed.

"You durn kids get out of here!" Mam'Ella hollered at the door. "What do you think you're doing in here?"

We scattered.

MaDear provided me with an easy audience to report what I had seen out in the world. With all this new information—sounds, accents, and images flooding into my brain—memories of our first home and my hometown were slipping away fast. MaDear rarely talked about our life before California, and that helped dim my memories, too. She was never chatty. The sharing of family stories was never her thing. She never talked about "back home" or her childhood in Arkansas. Her communication with her mother was limited to just a few words. I never found her gossiping with a neighbor or making cooing sounds with a baby. She was as silent and observant as a sphinx. Sometimes we kids would be talking about all kinds of things, thinking she was dozing on the couch or on her bed. Then later, she'd comment on something we'd said, dispossess us of our secrets, or shock us all by telling our grandmother who *really* broke something. My mother had always been there and, in so many ways, not there.

Whenever I misbehaved—talked back, moved too slowly when summoned, didn't complete an assigned chore—Mam'Ella, our new disciplinarian, would demand that I go find a belt. Every swish of the belt was accompanied by a word.

"When. I. Tell. You. To. Do. Something. You. Better. Do. It."

I'd reach out for my grandmother's arm to try to curb some of the force of each strike, and like that we'd dance around the parlor, performing some herky-jerky dance, but, despite all my efforts to ease the pain, she managed to get her licks in.

At some point, Mam'Ella started giving me a choice: a whipping or a punishment of staying indoors for days on end. I did the calculation: a whipping would take only a few minutes, and if I cried quickly and loudly enough, feigning contrition, the whole operation would be over in a snap. But the punishment of having to stay inside for one or two days was torture for a girl like me, who wanted nothing more than fresh air and freedom. There was too much to see for me to pass up an opportunity to get out of the house.

One day Albert and I had done something Mam'Ella deemed intolerable, and she demanded a belt to rectify the situation. She was going to "fix our red wagon," as she put it. Slowly, I went to my closet to find the skinniest belt available. The belt from a dress would be almost useless, so I scanned for one of those. But there were no belts in our closet. There were no belts in the dresser drawers either. I even went into my grandmother's room to fetch one of her thin dress belts, but I couldn't find one. I looked in Albert and Calvin's room, sure I'd find one there—boys always wore belts. Thick leather ones, unfortunately. But no belts.

My grandmother was in the kitchen, steaming with anger, claiming we were stalling on purpose. Then *she* went to look for a belt and she couldn't locate one either. She was furious, muttering under her breath, "These durn kids gonna drive me crazy!"

A few days later, I went into the kitchen to iron a dress for my mother. I pulled open the door to the ironing board closet and out fell every belt in the house—leather belts and plastic belts and fabric-fronted belts. Surprised, I started to laugh. I called Albert into the kitchen to come see, and he smiled, satisfied, and went back to what he was doing. I looked over at our mother, who sat at the table nursing a cup of coffee. As I stood there with a mass of belts in my hands, MaDear looked at me and a slight smile crept onto her face.

It was then that I remembered the morning of the belt search. My mother, through it all, hadn't said a word, hadn't protested on our behalf or helped search for belts or volunteered to punish us herself. She had just sat there, silent, nursing her coffee and smoking her Lucky Strikes. And now she sat in the same spot with that Mona Lisa smile of hers that seemed to say, "You're still my child and I won't let anyone harm you." This small conspiratorial act lifted my spirits for a long time. She had lost her sovereignty over us, her youngest children, but she hadn't surrendered her concern. I loved her for that.

My grandmother, the formidable Ella Baskin.

In our first couple years in California my grandmother, a dyed-in-the-wool Baptist, tried to honor my nuclear family's Catholic faith by sending Albert and me to St. Agnes Church on Masonic. It was clear to me from the start that Mam'Ella wanted me to be "good," but I had no idea exactly what that required of me. I never could understand all of her churchgoing and how long the services dragged on. There was church on Sunday, usher board meetings on Tuesday, and all kinds of committee meetings throughout the week. Then Sunday would roll around again. In the Catholic Church, you're in and out in an hour. It seemed to me that whatever you had to say to God or Jesus could surely be said in that amount of time. But churchgoing was sacrosanct to Mam'Ella. Crabbing about it got me nowhere. Mam'Ella had rules, and her *rules* had rules.

On the mantel in our living room rested a small rectangular plywood plaque that had the image of a doghouse painted on the left side. A small nail was driven in the door. Along the other side of the plaque was a row of five nails, from which hung five little wooden dog figures, each painted to look like a different breed. Each dog had the name of one of my uncles and aunts. Whenever my grandmother's children would piss her off, she would hang the corresponding dog figure in the doghouse. That was her silent notice that they had done something wrong. The dogs were in steady rotation, and I was fascinated to watch the revolving shame. My mother was the only one who didn't have a dog. To me that was both a source of pride and an insult.

As much as Mam'Ella wanted to influence me, I wanted to get her to see all the wonders I was discovering out in the world. There was something about her—was it her age, her Southern background, her religion?—that made her resist fun. She didn't play marbles or make crafts or do anything I'd call creative. She made me wonder where my mother had learned to do all the creative things, like making plastic lanyards, that I found most fun about her. One day I managed to pull Mam'Ella into the hippie shop on Cole and Carl, where people gave you merchandise—lamps, bread boxes, vases, macramé plant hangers, all kinds of stuff—for free. I had my eyes and heart set on a real, live cat I saw in the window. I had had a cat in St. Louis, a scrappy butterscotch cat that lived outdoors and was, for all intents and purposes, feral, but Albert and I claimed him as our own. We named him Tom.

Mam'Ella entered the place with caution. I watched as her eyes darted around to the pots and pans, ceramic knickknacks, the racks of floral maxi dresses, patchwork suede jackets, and crocheted ponchos. She inched her way around the store, picking up a few items, then putting them down carefully. The notion of a store giving away anything for free was admittedly strange, and I could tell she was suspicious of the whole operation. Mam'Ella was none too fond of the hippies in the neighborhood. She didn't trust them.

Around white people in general she always seemed to check herself, draw in, twist her Southern tongue to try and sound "proper." She often said, "What will white folks think?" whenever someone did or said something questionable, which made me wonder if it was white approval that we should be seeking as we moved through the world. I would come to realize only later that she was telling me that white people were always analyzing us, judging our behavior, sometimes harshly and with horrible consequences. But on this day, the hippies' intent was clear—everything in this store was free—so why not take advantage?

"See, Mam'Ella. I can have that cat for free." I pointed to the animal, who came toward us as we approached its cage and pressed his nose against the bars. It was an off-white kitten with just a hint of gray dusting its fur and black stripes crossing the length of its body.

My grandmother scowled at the cat as I stroked its shoulder.

"I ain't never seen no cat like that."

"It's cute, huh."

I liked old Tom fine, but this cat . . . this cat I *knew* I could really love!

"What kinda cat is that?"

I pulled out of my reverie to read the card attached to the front of the cage. Hmm. A word I didn't know. I studied it for a moment, then turned triumphantly to Mam'Ella.

"It's an oc-e-lot!" I said, sure that I was correct in my pronunciation.

Mam'Ella frowned. "A what?!"

I repeated, "Ocelot." I read the rest of the card. "Exotic. Native to Mexico and South America."

My grandmother turned toward the door.

"Girl, come out of here. That thing gon' turn into a tiger when it gets big! Eat up everybody in the house."

All my protests about the store being free and cats making good pets—quiet and self-cleaning—fell on deaf ears. Mam'Ella was not having it. I did not know it then, but my new California family was afraid of cats, had all kinds of superstitions about them that I had never heard, like cats "taking baby's breath." I was crestfallen.

I walked past the store a few days later to pet the cat and watch it move its small, rubbery body around the cage, but a week later it was gone. Someone else had lucked out.

Some days I'd sneak away from the kids on Cole Street and trek alone to Golden Gate Park after school to watch the hippies sing, chant, smoke pot, and blow soap bubbles while some long-haired troubadour played guitar. I was witnessing the ragged end of something wonderful and revolutionary, but I didn't know that then. I figured the neighborhood had always been this way. The

Haight-Ashbury hippies fascinated me. Their Summer of Love had morphed into something bedraggled and forlorn and desperate. I had never seen so many young white people in tattered, mismatched clothes and greasy hair. Actually, I had never seen anybody in such a state. There was a hippie kid in my class, Donovan, who went barefoot whenever he wasn't in school. He came to class with uncombed, tangled hair and a dirty face and hands, like no one cared about him at all. His hippie parents smelled of patchouli oil and cloves—scents I'd never get used to. Donovan never seemed to have a care in the world. The hippies weren't like the tidy white folks on TV who were scrubbed clean, pressed and polished. The Haight-Ashbury crew helped me understand better than anything else in my life up to that point that the world of TV was a myth, and that there were any number of types of "normal." I studied the hippies, more curious than afraid. Thinking they were in need of real help, I asked Mam'Ella about them one day.

My grandmother humphed and wrinkled her nose. "You don't worry about them kids. Shoot, some of those kids' mamas and daddies working at the university over in Berkeley. They runaways. They not poor. Naw, naw. They not poor. Just putting it on for a while."

Why, I wondered, would anyone in their right mind *pretend* to be poor and live on the streets if they didn't have to? I was too young to understand what freedoms the hippies sought when they landed in the Haight-Ashbury. What could be denied white people, after all? What had they expected to find here in our neighborhood? What would make them want to escape their families and comfortable homes to come to this place that had lost its luster? As we passed young men nodding in doorways and young women begging for change, offering us daisy wreaths to put in our hair, I sensed that these kids—and they were, behind all the grime and scabs and bravado, just kids—were searching for something important, meaningful. They wanted answers just like I did. I just couldn't figure out what their questions could be.

In our first couple years in California my grandmother tried to honor my nuclear family's Catholic faith by sending Albert and me to St. Agnes Church on Masonic. Mam'Ella would always give us a few coins to contribute to the offering plate, but it didn't take long before we realized that the Catholic Church had enough money, so Albert suggested we spend our money on candy and soda instead. Laura Scudder's BBQ potato chips and Tahitian Treat soda were much tastier than that single flavorless wafer. On more than a few Sundays we didn't make it to St. Agnes at all but instead tucked into a storefront "hippie church" where the minister preached a gospel of peace and love and passed out tiny cups of Mogen David wine, which I mistook for grape juice. Instead of hymns, the congregation sang folk songs, accompanied by guitars and tambourines. They hugged each other a lot and talked about our souls and the energy we all emit and how that energy could impact the world. They didn't speak of original sin or damnation to a fiery hell, like the preacher at Mam'Ella's church. The hippies spoke of having your spirit nourished. They said they wanted peace. I liked them for that. Passing them on the street, they'd often throw me the peace sign and smile.

"Peace, little one."

And I'd respond in kind: "Peace."

five
WAR ON PINE

At the end of fourth grade, our family pulled up stakes again and moved from my beloved Cole Street. I had to say goodbye to Stephanie and Hap, the hippies, and all the other kids in the neighborhood to start over again elsewhere. We moved to Pine Street, where there were hardly any hippies, hardly any kids, and lots of westbound traffic. There was no more playing in the street. No more friends either. It was one of the quietest residential areas I had ever been in. The house at 2825 Pine Street was a tall, lean, darkly painted Victorian with tall double front doors with colored-glass panes. A skylight right in the middle of the house shone brightly in an area that, like a spoke of a wagon wheel, connected the parlor, bedrooms, bathroom, and kitchen. Off the large kitchen, at the rear of the house, was a big sun porch that provided views of similarly lean houses. It was the grandest house I'd ever been in, like something in an old Vincent Price horror movie. The parlor, where most of our non-eating activities occurred, was trimmed in a dark wainscotting that gave off an oppressive feeling, and an old-timey chandelier hung high up above us.

I was being called on to start again, to be the new girl, the new student, the new neighbor. I wondered how many new versions of myself I could muster in a lifetime. Would I be like a cat with nine lives? I would have to see. That first summer in the Western Addition neighborhood, I watched endless hours of AAU track and field trials, toying with the dream of becoming a sprinter. I had my doubts of making it on to the US team, however, as my legs had begun to hurt all the time.

Mam'Ella told me, "That's just growing pains. They'll go away."

But I wasn't so sure.

On July 20, 1969, I sat on the floor close to the television to watch the Apollo 11 moon landing. Mam'Ella, sitting in her afghan-covered recliner behind me, watched, too. She sucked her teeth and spit out a stream of tobacco juice into her Maxwell House coffee can. We listened intently as Walter Cronkite narrated the extraordinary scene with such gravitas that I was sucked in completely, wondering why anyone would want to go to the moon. What did they hope to find there? Nothing looked like what we saw on *Lost in Space* or *Star Trek*. Everything was grainy and dark and, well, lunar.

"That is fake! Ain't nobody gone to no moon!" Mam'Ella said.

Still, I was riveted, waiting for something dramatic to happen. Would an alien suddenly appear? And what would Neil Armstrong do if one did?

"That's Hollywood," she said loudly a moment later.

"No, it's not," I finally said. "It's NASA. It's real. They said in school that it was gonna happen."

"It's not real. It's a TV show, trying to make us believe they on the moon."

"Why would anybody do that?" I asked, turning around to look at her. "It's not even good TV," I said, turning back to the screen. "Besides, the president knows about it. *And* Walter Cronkite." I added this bit because I knew Walter Cronkite was my grandmother's respected oracle of information. His word was gospel.

But Ella Baskin refused to relent. No man can go to the moon, she said, much less walk on it. I kept watching anyway as the astronaut bounced upon the pitted landscape, tethered like a helium balloon to his spacecraft. As my grandmother looked at the television with suspicion, I looked at her with the same wariness, wondering how she could believe in heaven and not a man on the moon.

Eventually she got up from her recliner, gave a final grunt at the television, and, as she walked out of the room, said, "What you don't know will make a whole new world."

I had no doubt about that. This statement was meant to humble me, but it only emboldened me to learn more about the world.

That fall Mam'Ella enrolled me in Emerson School on Scott and California Streets, but I wasn't there long. Shortly after my enrollment my teacher requested a conference with Mam'Ella. As I often did, I accompanied my grandmother to the school and was therefore part of the meeting. The teacher asked Mam'Ella if I had skipped a grade. Not knowing the answer, she turned to me. Confused by the concept, I shook my head.

"No," Mam'Ella told the teacher, who, in turn, said that I was very smart and that she was considering recommending me for promotion to sixth grade, but the school needed Mam'Ella's permission, as she was my legal guardian.

My grandmother, who by now made all decisions about our care and education, refused to consent. "No need to bother," is how she put it.

"If she's supposed to be in fifth grade," my grandmother said, "keep her there."

I had not thought about sixth grade, what it might feel like, how I might fare in it, but once the possibility was presented and then rejected, I felt slighted. My grandmother had just deprived me of something I didn't even know I wanted until it was no longer available. And there was nothing I could do about it, and nothing my mother could do about it either, as she no longer had power in her family, no sway with her mother. Seeing my mother powerless compounded my powerlessness, made me feel vulnerable. I came to realize that year, in many discomfiting ways, that I was no longer my mother's child. Sure, I called her MaDear and looked like her and presented her with her favorite coconut candy bar on Mother's Day, but she had been divested of all maternal responsibilities. She couldn't help me navigate my way through the world; she knew too little of it. Too bad, too, because I'm sure she would have let me go on to the sixth grade. In a snap.

About a month or so into the school year, I was pulled from

class along with a few other students. We were told that we'd be bussed to Winfield Scott Elementary School, in the Marina District. I had no idea where that was, or why we in particular were being bussed there, but I got the impression that the teachers wanted us to look at this as an opportunity.

On the daily school bus ride to Winfield Scott Elementary, Negro faces quickly disappeared from the streets as we crested the hill into tony Pacific Heights and then descended into the lily-white Cow Hollow and Marina districts. No lesson I learned or teacher's name from that experience survives in my memory; I only remember the feeling of self-consciousness, much like the feeling I had when I'd first arrived at St. Vincent's Day Home. I didn't think of this as a great educational or social opportunity. I didn't think about white kids from Winfield Scott being transported to Emerson. I didn't fully understand why I got picked to leave my neighborhood school, which was only a few blocks from our house, to trek to a school two or three neighborhoods away. If I was smart, and I believed I was, why couldn't I be smart in my neighborhood school? Whatever they had at Winfield Scott, why couldn't Emerson have the same thing? The effort all seemed like a great waste of time and gas.

One day after school, I stalled getting on the big yellow bus and suggested to the driver that I could very easily walk home. It would be easy. Just straight up Divisadero and turn right on Pine Street. Easy as pie. I was intrigued by the unbelievable pitch of the hill. Could I climb that hill? But the bus driver gave me a flat, "No, get on the bus." Clearly he was not impressed with my keen navigational skills. As the bus passed the tile-roofed Mediterranean houses of the

Marina District and the sprawling multilevel mansions of Pacific Heights, with their breathtaking views of San Francisco Bay, I knew that I didn't belong in the Marina District. What was the point of sending me to a place I wasn't even allowed to walk out of? No one, at that point, had explained that great social experiment of school bussing to me. What I knew about it was only what I had seen on television in news reports from the South, which always included the ugly, violent efforts some people made to avoid it at all costs.

Not long after the start of the school year, I was pulled abruptly from Winfield Scott School and enrolled at St. Dominic's School, five blocks down Pine Street from our house. Hallelujah! No more getting up early to catch a bus, to pick out and iron school clothes. I'd be back in a hassle-free parochial school uniform and able to walk to school. I took life's little conveniences as they came to me. All except one.

Mam'Ella took me one day to the barbershop around the corner on Bush Street and instructed the barber to cut my hair.

The barber regarded me a bit tentatively, then said, "Are you sure, Mrs. Baskin? She's a little girl."

My grandmother assured him that she knew I was a girl and that she wanted him to cut my hair, which hadn't grown very much since my days at St. Vincent's but was now long enough to pull into a little ponytail. This request was a radical move for the time, not just because these were press-and-curl days but because little Black girls didn't wear short Afros, or any kind of Afros in those days. These were "sit in the kitchen on a Saturday night and have your mother, aunt, or grandmother put a hot comb on the stove, grease your scalp with Royal Crown Hair Dressing or Dixie Peach, and get your hair pressed" days. If you came from a family with money, your mother could send you to a salon, where you'd learn from the women there how to press and style your hair, how to gossip, and how to ingest an aesthetic of beauty that was as unnatural as walking on the moon. Little girls had braids, ribbons, and barrettes. A finely coiffed head meant someone cared about you and how you were viewed in the world; it meant someone paid attention.

Reluctantly, the barber did as instructed. He cut my hair down low. A boy's haircut. As I silently watched my hair fall on the barber's drape and down to the floor, I felt a little like Samson must have felt, losing his hair, losing his power.

I was enrolled in Mrs. Velasquez's class at St. Dominic's School. She was my first teacher who wasn't white. Like Mr. Eckart, she was a nice teacher and kept an orderly classroom. After nearly two years in public school, I had almost forgotten the rigid schedule and features of a Catholic school. Mass every day at noon. A tiny playground. Watchful nuns. No cafeteria.

After school I headed straight home. On Cole Street kids seemed to pour out of houses, but Pine Street was as barren as the Sahara. On Pine Street it felt like everyone I could make friends with lived on the other side of Geary Boulevard. We lived on the northwestern edge of the Western Addition district. I had grown tired of riding my bike all the way back to the Haight-Ashbury to play with my old friends. Usually by the time I got over there, their mothers would be calling them in for dinner and I'd be encouraged to get home. Meanwhile, my cousin Donna and her family had moved from Shrader Street to Oakland, where the rest of my mother's siblings lived, so I was left to my own devices, to drum up entertainment for myself.

Juanita, a girl from my class, was the only kid I knew who lived nearby. She was pretty, with long black wavy hair that was always neatly gathered into two tightly braided ropes. She lived around the corner on California Street. One day she invited me over to play, and I, desperate for friends, accepted the invitation. I knew that she bullied kids in the class, but I was so lonely I set my caution aside. After school I proudly announced to my mother when she asked where I was going that I had a new friend named Juanita and I was going to play with her.

As soon as I got to Juanita's house, I didn't feel good about it. She was swinging on her family's big redwood fence that stretched across their driveway, hanging over it like a cat. She didn't jump down when I arrived. And I just stood there, waiting for something to happen—a jump rope competition, a game of checkers or jacks, an invitation to race to the end of the block. Something. Juanita gave me nothing. Instead she started to call me names. She told me that I was a dumb, ugly girl. Bald-headed. This stung because people visiting our house or stopping to talk to my grandmother on the street often confused me for a boy. I had nothing against boys, but I never wanted people to think I was one either.

Juanita said that no one wanted to be my friend. Not her, not anyone.

"Why'd you come over here? I don't like you."

I don't think she could have strung any other words together that could have hurt more than those. I had been to three schools that year and had finally felt I would be able to settle down and make some real friends to replace the ones I missed so much back on Cole Street. But to Juanita I was a joke, a piece of dirt that you could kick off the soles of your shoes.

I don't remember saying anything to Juanita. Her message was clear. I headed to the fence that swung out over the sidewalk. I grabbed the end of it that latched onto the post and, with both hands and all my might, I swung it shut and sent nasty Juanita flying backward toward her garage door. I didn't stick around to find out where or how Juanita landed. I ran back to Pine Street, terrified at the anger that welled up inside me, and back to my mother, who was a far better companion than I ever found at St. Dominic's.

Juanita never bothered me again, but my experience with her left me wondering if pummeling someone was the only way to deal with bullies.

Every night MaDear, Mam'Ella, and I watched the six o'clock news.

"Turn on Walter Cronkite," my grandmother would say, accepting no substitutes.

The main story was about another, far more significant war: Vietnam. The conflict began nearly every evening broadcast, and it dominated the front page of the newspaper daily.

What You Don't Know Will Make a Whole New World

Mr. Cronkite and other TV reporters braved sniper fire, bombings, and grenade attacks to tell us about the war and America's diminishing chances of winning it. It wasn't ever clear to me why we were fighting in Southeast Asia in the first place, just that we were paying a heavy toll being there. This was the first time that I witnessed scenes of real suffering not just from the soldiers, many of whom were Black and so young, but from Vietnamese villagers who were being terrorized and slaughtered. I wondered why we couldn't beat the Vietnamese without the napalm. This didn't seem like the honorable fight that was always depicted in the World War II movies. Why were we fighting peasants instead of soldiers? What kind of people did this make us?

These nightly newscasts were my first lessons about America's foreign policy and military might. This war—it took no time to realize—was not about the spit-and-polish, valiant military of the movies, where decisions were made quickly and "our" aims were black-and-white. In the movies, there was only honor and glory in being a soldier. And the US was always right. This war, this real war in Vietnam, was far more muddy, bloody, and complicated. Its moral and political implications were as dense as the jungles the soldiers fought and died in.

I was learning that there were many layers of peace. There was the peace that the hippies wanted—to just get along with everybody and not be hassled by people who chose to live differently than they did. There was peace that church folk talked about—having God in their lives. And there was peace that antiwar protesters demanded of their government.

Violence seemed to creep into all corners of life during my fifth-grade year. The neighborhood in those days felt devoid of young men; so many of them had been drafted and shipped out to Vietnam. My one male cousin who was of draft age—but was apolitical and certainly not college-bound—had no involvement in the war, and my brother Albert, sixteen at the time, had been shipped to Washington state for a stint in Job Corps, so it seemed he was safe, at least for the time being. Knowing that he would not be around to be drafted made me feel safe, and that was worth something. Besides, MaDear assured me, he had had tuberculosis as a kid, so his bad lungs would surely keep him out of the draft.

Still, war was ever-present. Since our arrival in California, we had watched a steady diet of large and small wars. We saw student protests and race riots. Bottles hurled on Paris boulevards. Tanks rolling down cobbled Prague streets. Fists raised on Olympic victory stands. Violence was no stranger in our house either. My cousin Ed was shot one night, sending our grandmother into hysterics and out into the night to San Francisco General. Mam'Ella was also battling with a wild, unruly teenaged foster child named Toni, whom she had to physically tussle with on occasion. It seemed everybody was warring for control of somebody or something—a country's resources, a government, a classroom, or a curfew. People were always fighting each other for something they felt was theirs to control—tangible things like land, and intangible things like honor and decency.

six

WESTERN ADDITION

M am'Ella stood at the back door, bellowing my full name.
I was right under the porch, standing with my back flush
against the house, in the asphalt triangle of our backyard. In this
restricted place I attempted to train Pepe, the black terrier my
grandmother had adopted. I dreamed up imaginary playmates. I
recreated scenes from TV shows. I sang all the songs I knew.

My grandmother called me again. "Dorothy Ann Lazard!"

Acting deaf was a game I played *on*, but not *with*, my grandmother. I knew if my whole name was called, the time for play was
over. My grandmother meant business. But I always took my time
going up the stairs. Sloth was my small act of rebellion.

"Huh?"

"What?! Don't you say 'huh' to me," she said, holding the back
door open. "Or 'what,'" she added, referring to my regular alterna-
tive to "huh."

Once we were inside, she gave me my assignment: "I want you to write me a letter."

I followed her through the kitchen to the living room, where she took a seat in her recliner. I sat on the ottoman at her knee.

"I want you to write a letter to Lula Belle."

Mam'Ella regularly commissioned me to write letters not only to Lula Belle and other distant relatives in Chicago but to her insurance company, the phone company, and to Reverend Ike, a radio evangelist to whom she regularly sent money orders.

We had a rhythm, my grandmother and I. We'd take our places. She would gaze out the window at the slice of daylight that wedged itself between our bay window and that of the house next door, and then she'd begin her narration. Ever so often she'd spit a brown stream of Day's Work tobacco juice into a Maxwell House coffee can.

If the letter was directed to family members, you could bet money that it would begin the same way each time: "Dear _____, How are you? Fine, I hope. It has been such a long time since I heard from you." Then she'd proceed with news of various relatives, like who in the family had just had a baby or who had just recovered from an illness. She'd end with "Yours truly, Ella." A stamp would be affixed to the envelope and off the letter would go.

Bored with the orthodoxy of this task, and flushed with a secret desire to have my own letters to write, I sometimes wandered off the beaten track, adding my own words here and there.

"Read it back to me," my grandmother said.

Out of the corner of my eye, I saw the Maxwell House coffee can rise and then lower slowly. Read it back to her? She had never asked this before. Recently I had been adding a word or two of my own to the letters. Instead of the usual opening of "How are you? Fine, I hope," I had been writing the more extravagant "I hope this letter finds you in good health and spirits," or "Good fortune has visited us since my last letter to you." It had gone undetected for several weeks before this latest letter to Lula Belle, so I had grown quite comfortable accessorizing my grandmother's dictation.

My grandmother wiped her chin with the edge of her apron. "Well, go on."

I cleared my throat.

"Read it," she commanded.

"'Dear Lula Belle,'" I began. Fidgeting, I proceeded to read my composition, sliding the ottoman a couple of feet away from the recliner as I did. The letter was a pretty fair representation of what she had said, but then I read the last lines, which went something like, "Send everyone our best wishes. Tell them that they are in our prayers." My grandmother frowned. Over her bifocals, anchored by the large black mole on her nose, she peered at me with suspicion.

"What was that last part?"

"Yours truly, Ella," I said.

"No. Before that."

"Oh." I took a deep breath, half expecting to be batted on my ear. I repeated my closing remarks.

"I didn't say nothin' like that," she said.

I kept quiet; no need to dispute the obvious.

"Why'd you put that in there when I didn't say it? You're writing a letter for *me*, remember."

What You Don't Know Will Make a Whole New World

"Yes, ma'am."

Quickly I rewrote the letter before her original dull remarks escaped me. For the rest of the evening my grandmother sent me disapproving looks over her glasses, but she said nothing more about my transgression. Realizing I had done something to unsettle her thrilled me. She didn't know it, but these minor acts of subversion were fueled by clandestine visits to the local public library.

The Western Addition branch library on Geary Boulevard and Scott was where I discovered a world I hadn't imagined before. With each book I read, my perceptions ballooned. In my house there were only two things to read besides the daily *San Francisco Examiner*: my grandmother's Bible and old copies of *Jet* magazine, a miniature tabloid filled cover to cover with celebrity gossip, society weddings, and political news. The Bible seemed too forbidding with all of its tiny print and odd names. And *Jet* . . . well, *Jet* never held my attention past the TV listings of upcoming shows featuring Black performers. But like so many other grandmothers in the neighborhood, mine swore by both publications.

At the library that year I read *The Autobiography of Malcolm X* and learned that during his incarceration Malcolm had copied a page from the dictionary every day. He was what people called an autodidact, a self-taught person. And I wanted to become one, too. The library was a great, seductive classroom, fueling in me tactile and cerebral longings. Hungrily I read snatches of every book I touched. I read reviews on the back covers of paperbacks, first paragraphs, last sentences. I was fascinated by the variety of cover designs, type styles, chapter headings, and titles. It seemed to me that I could live forever, reading every day, all day, and still not read everything in that branch library. The concept was overwhelming, troubling, and tantalizing. Each time I learned a new word or noticed how a writer cobbled sentences together, what diction she used, I felt like fireworks were going off in my head. British writers, I noticed, spelled words differently from American writers. "Parlour" instead of "parlor." "Apologise" instead of "apologize." They loved adverbs and used them to great effect. There were a thousand species of plant life and landscapes I didn't know—yew trees, moors, sycamores, heather. I discovered that many of the movies I loved had begun life as books, and I bounced my way through many of them. The children's books came in so many sizes and shapes they created a mess on the shelves. One of my favorites was *Ticonderoga Tales*, a book so tall and narrow that it had to be tipped on its side to fit on the shelves, and still it was a trip hazard.

Always a daydreamer, I was supplied with fresh fodder at the library. I could spend the afternoon being an inventor, a prairie farmer, a runaway slave. I read *The Thin Man* and fancied myself a detective. *The Diary of a Young Girl*, about Anne Frank hiding with her family in an attic to escape Nazi torture, made me rethink all those World War II movies I had watched that focused on the soldiers, never the kids. I learned a bit about the French Revolution from Alexandre Dumas and the power and variety of poetry from Langston Hughes. I discovered *Freedom Train*, Dorothy Sterling's biography of Harriet Tubman, which sparked a lifelong obsession with the famed abolitionist and with runaways in general.

Most significantly, I found Black women writers—Maya Angelou, Toni Morrison, and Virginia Hamilton—who spoke about things in a language I recognized. I'll never forget the feeling of exhilaration that came over me when I read Black dialect for the first time. It was like being in a room with family members. Seeing words in print that had only existed for me in spoken language was validating. Seeing them in books somehow made what I had experienced feel significant. And I realized that Black girls could grow up to become writers of books housed in libraries. What a powerful thing! Who ever knew?!

Even more delicious was the fact that my grandmother didn't know about my library excursions. It was a part of my life she did not control. When the three o'clock bell rang and the children of St. Dominic's School scattered like buckshot through the neighborhood, I headed directly home to do chores, but the magic time after chores and before dinner was all mine. My grandmother hardly ever asked me where I was going—as long as I was back well before dark, as long as my chores were done. My mother, on the other hand, was eager for me to head outside. A trip out of the house meant that she'd be rewarded later with a story of what I saw or did. The sooner I got home from school and tended to any of my mother's needs (pills, sandwich, coffee, cigarette, TV, chat), the sooner I could leave.

My grandmother, however, was suspicious of anything that set one apart from industry and family. That included what she called "book-learning." When I finally bolstered the nerve to present my grandmother with a library card application, she asked: "How much does this cost?"

"The library is free."

"How much do the books cost if you lose one?"

I couldn't say. I didn't think to ask, but I swore I wouldn't lose any. I told her I was really good at dates and that I'd make sure to return them on time. Still, she refused.

Fortunately, whatever disappointment I felt about her refusal didn't last. I liked going to the library to do my reading anyway. It was quiet there, and no one expected anything of me but to read. Among the community of readers, I felt like a serious reader myself. It was during this honeymoon with the public library that I began to see how my life could be radically different from my mother's and grandmother's lives. It was a little bit frightening, but exciting, too. I could be my own something if I only learned enough. I just needed to find out what there was to learn.

Our family had no legacy of higher education or working professionals. We were a blue-collar family. I never got a sense that MaDear liked school or had had much experience there.

"I passed by the schoolhouse door" was about all she regularly said about her own education. I knew she hadn't finished high school, having married and started a family by sixteen. But her pride in my scholastic achievements was full-bodied and accompanied by treats.

What You Don't Know Will Make a Whole New World

My grandmother, on the other hand, felt something closer to tolerance than pride for my love of learning. Ella Baskin was a practical woman who had worked hard all her life. She had picked cotton in the South, worked as a maid, a nurse's aide, and several other things. Her sense of self was rooted in work and the ability to provide for her family. She had no time for book-spun dreams or remote possibilities. Books were for "people with too much time on their hands," I heard her say more than a few times. Anybody worth her salt was working, not sitting around with her nose in a book.

Knowing she felt this way, I was not about to share my budding desire to become a writer. How worthless would she think writers were if *books* were a waste of time? It seemed as though she may have looked at owning books and having time to read them as a luxury she could not afford to indulge in. Everything she needed to know, Mam'Ella used to tell me, was in her Bible or learned through experience. Common sense vs. book sense. Silently I disagreed; books had already taught me better than that. But I saw no reason to try to change her mind.

One day when I came home, bragging about the good grade I had received on some assignment, my grandmother said, "Boys won't like you if you're too smart," which left me wondering how smart was "too smart." Maybe a book in the library could tell me. Absorbing words like dry soil in a rainstorm, I sensed that the more I learned, the more I was moving, slowly but surely, toward something fulfilling. I began to see ignorance as a kind of poverty. What might my mother's life be like if she was educated? For that matter, how might her children's lives or her mother's be different?

At the library, other readers egged on my new obsession. I watched what books adults pulled from the shelves. Sometimes they'd tell me the plots of books they had read, and, based on what they said, I would determine whether or not the books were worth my time. The librarian must have known that the books I pored over were way beyond my comprehension, but she never steered me back to the children's section. On the contrary, she suggested that I get a library card so I could take books home. I confused her by declining her offer, observing the stalemate at my house.

This new appetite of mine reached a fever pitch when my older sister Sarah came to California from Chicago to attend nursing school. Ten years my senior, Sarah was my mother's third child from her first marriage, the child my father reared after our mother's first marriage dissolved. Like the Gold Rush pioneers we had learned about in fourth grade, Sarah had heard California was a land of opportunity, a great place to get a good education and make a new life. Convinced by our grandmother that school was cheap in California, Sarah arrived in San Francisco full of hope, radical ideas, and Smokey Robinson and the Miracles albums. Her hair was an explosion of Black Power—a big Afro style that made me feel a little less self-conscious about my own lost hair. She owned a copy of Mao's *Little Red Book*, and loudly condemned the Vietnam War. She was a radical in our midst, like the ones we saw on TV. Sarah blew a breath of youthful, unpredictable vigor into our quiet Victorian. Unlike my mother, my grandmother needed no medication to soothe what ailed her; she needed order.

Order didn't come.

When Sarah found out I liked to read but had no library card, she made sure I got one. To my relief, the librarian didn't ask any questions when Sarah nonchalantly signed the library application. The librarian simply typed out our cards and handed them over to us with a smile. I felt like a real citizen then with my first city-administered membership card.

Sarah had very particular tastes in books. Mysteries, romances, histories, poetry, and gothic tales by Edgar Allan Poe were her favorites. She was the first avid reader I knew.

Sister Sarah, an inspiring, stabilizing force in my life, who taught me the liberating power of books.

She introduced me to Shakespeare's sonnets, the Nancy Drew series, Paul Laurence Dunbar's poetry (which she could recite by heart), and Eldridge Cleaver's *Soul on Ice*, which I crawled through, confused and slightly horrified to find curse words in print.

With Sarah as my first reader's advisory, I was suddenly in book heaven. I wanted to become her literary comrade in the house, someone with whom I not only read books but discussed them. Sarah tried to explain to me alien concepts like colonialism, Pan-Africanism, and the conjugation of French verbs. Once she began school, she brought home history books and anatomy textbooks. She had a copy of *Everything You Ever Wanted to Know About Sex (But Were Afraid to Ask)*, and, with it, I discovered my own anatomy. As my view of the world expanded, so did my view of my-self and my place in it. My notion of education was forever altered that year, and, as a result, so was school's relevance.

My household obligations took on a growing insignificance.

After reading Louise Fitzhugh's children's novel *Harriet the Spy*, I took to roaming my neighborhood, pretending to be a detective like the main character. In a small steno pad I jotted descriptions of how people spoke, ate, and held their cigarettes; how fog rolled in from the west; how the elderly lugged themselves and their par-cels around. It was fun to watch life in all its varied details go on around me. I felt my senses developing, like muscles being toned.

One day while I was playing with Pepe in the backyard, enjoy-ing a swatch of rare afternoon sun, my grandmother called me in.

"Hey, come in here!"

I saw the top of her head as she leaned over the banister. "You hear me! I know you're down there."

When I reached her on the sun porch, I saw she was holding my rumpled notebook. "What's this?" she asked. Her smirk let me know that she was in no mood for half-baked answers or sullen si-lence.

"That's *my* notebook," I said, more defensively than I intended.

"What is this you're writing in here? About me and folks at my church." She flipped through the pages. "See, here's my name: 'Ella puts on her white usher board uniform and white shoes and heads to church every Sunday at the same time.'"

I couldn't figure out why she was so angry. I hadn't misrepresented her. What was so bad about me noticing her? She went on, pointing out names of familiar people and places.

"Why are you taking this down?"

Even though I had pretended to be a spy, I figured my grandmother must know—how could she think otherwise?—that these were only harmless notes. Descriptive phrases that became sentences, seeds to stories I would write for my backyard audience of one. Surely, I thought, she couldn't believe I was a *real* spy!

"I was just writing," I said. "They're just notes."

"But for what? Why did you put my name on this paper?"

I shrugged.

That was enough to set her off. She reached for the fly swatter, the nearest weapon she could find, and popped me a few times on my bare legs. Tears came, but not from any pain inflicted by the fly swatter. I cried because, once she put the fly swatter away, she peeled off page after page from my notebook and ripped each one into shreds.

By destroying my first attempts at writing, though, my grandmother unwittingly lit a fire. Her act of intolerance was an important lesson about the power of words. There was something about what I had written that put her on the defensive, made her look at me differently, with a suspicion that, at least, promised engagement if not acceptance. Words written were exhilarating but costly. People who were committed to them paid a price, I was learning. And that price, I would realize later, is where great stories come from. With these words, set down so innocently, I was building a voice of my own, word by word, page by page. All learning is risk, for it is an admission that you don't know something and are willing to do whatever it takes to gain that knowledge, no matter the cost to ego, relationships, or expectations. Words that had lain so passively on pages before my relationship with the library now took on new meaning. Every word meant something, and together they could create storms, tirades, worry, suspicion. They could also liberate and weave fresh possibilities. All children have interior, secret lives, where their imaginations blossom and their perceptions of their worlds form. I was no different. As a reader, I was learning so much, but I somehow understood that not all of what I was learning should be shared. I knew, for instance, not to tell Mam'Ella that I did not believe in what they preached at her church. Religion, God, and the precepts of the church, I sensed, were inviolable to her, something not to be challenged. At least not out loud.

Mam'Ella's church, Ebenezer Baptist Church, was all fire and brimstone. There was a lot of talk about sin and evil and other scary things that would, as the old folks said, "put the fear of God in you." The church choir offered loud, thumping music that sent the women into a clapping, fanning, jumping frenzy, unlike anything I ever saw at the relatively solemn St. Agnes Catholic Church. At Ebenezer Baptist, I sat among the congregation, entranced by the display of emotion, the beseeching arms shot up to the sky, the frantic waves of funeral-home fans. The women mumbled "yes, Lawd"s and "amen"s. Whenever I was at Mam'Ella's church, I always felt as if Jesus had me by the scruff of my neck, shaking me like the nuns at St. Vincent's Day Home sometimes did. Mam'Ella seemed to be praying to a bully god who scared you into submission. If that was faith, I wanted no part of it.

The churchgoers, mostly women, had given themselves over to something I didn't understand or connect with emotionally. I didn't know if it was because I was Catholic and accustomed to a much more staid display of religious devotion or because I was truly a "sinner." But the spirit never grabbed hold of me. I found the stories the preacher told so disconnected from my experience. No one in Bible times, it seemed to me, was having any fun or living without a threat of some political, physical, or environmental danger. I didn't like the idea of original sin, of having been born with some mark already against me before I could even lift my own head! No part of my grandmother's worship felt gratifying or affirming. Everything good and fulfilling was coming "in the sweet by-and-by," once you got to heaven. *If* you got to heaven.

What's more, in my budding understanding of race, power, and Black history, I couldn't understand why my grandmother—why all our Christian elders—would pray to a white savior. How could she, coming from Southern sharecroppers who had sprung from slaves, make that okay? Hadn't we gotten this form of Christianity from slaveholders? Whenever Sarah said anything about our African heritage or about our slave ancestors, our grandmother would insist that *she* hadn't come from slaves or from Africans (which may explain why she always said after a busy day at work that she had been "working like a *Hebrew* slave" instead of an African one). She and Sarah had endless arguments about this. Mam'Ella found the whole notion of an African connection insulting. I was also confused by how she could square the self-sacrifice espoused in her church with the materialism promoted by Reverend Ike, the radio evangelist she followed regularly. He was not waiting for the sweet by-and-by. In his radio broadcasts, he preached a "get yours now" mantra. "It's better to have it and not need it than to need it and not have it," he often said.

At ten, I was already learning that life could dole out a mound of challenges and contradictions. I couldn't deal with the unfairness of being Black in America, a girl, a child of old and vulnerable parents, *and* considered a sinner. It was just too much to take on.

It was mainly the church music, especially the piano, that hooked me during the services. The piano seemed to penetrate not just my ears but my skin and go right into my heart. That, more than any sermon I heard, affected me, connected me to the people at the church. It gave me the first inkling that I had a soul to stir. Yet, I wondered if religion was just another form of slavery. I didn't dare ask Mam'Ella. I just kept reading.

I held libraries in the highest esteem. In what other city building could a ten-year-old go, unaccompanied, and wander freely? The Western Addition branch gave me an unexpected power. But a power, I realized, I didn't know what to do with. I decided that year that I would definitely become a writer. All these writers whose thoughts, ideas, life experiences, and labors were encased between innocuous book covers were once fifth-graders like me, with a desire for self-expression. The idea of observing and retelling something I'd observed had rattled my old granny. She couldn't articulate what bothered her about my notebook—to be fair, I couldn't either back then—but the fact that it had given her a conniption was wholly satisfying. Before I decided to become a writer, however, my first ambition was more fundamental: I just wanted to be smart. I wanted to know things, to be able to read books without a dictionary on my lap, to answer people's questions with ease.

As my vocabulary grew, as my sense of the world expanded, I realized that my education was setting me apart, forcing me to question just about everything in our lives. Including God.

I was becoming someone quite different from my grandmother.

The more suspicious my grandmother became of my early literary efforts, the greater the library's appeal grew. She took to rifling through my bookbag in search of written contraband. But, always, she came up empty-handed. I didn't give up my note-taking or my reading. My mother, silent during most of my conflicts with my grandmother, had privately presented me with a replacement notebook the week after my grandmother destroyed that first cherished one. Where she got it from I never knew, but I was grateful to receive it. This small conspiratorial act affirmed that she was still my mother, my savior.

Before I discovered the library, I had spent more time with my mother, and I had always been present and available to empty my grandmother's coffee can of tobacco slop; to help her at the board and care home she ran for developmentally disabled adults; and to write her letters. But, once I started to read in earnest, the library took possession of me. If there was a book nearby, I was as inattentive as a gnat. Pots burned, soups cooled, floors went half swept, dishes were left to soak. I stayed away from home as much as any ten-year-old could. Like a seed to sun, I pointed my head toward light.

After a few months of unrepentant library visits, both alone and with Sarah, I noticed that my grandmother had eased off me about my errant housekeeping. I learned to strike a balance between chores and reading that seemed to satisfy her. But the itch to write was growing.

One day a letter arrived from Chicago from another far-off relative. I carried it to my grandmother, who was busy at the board and care home across the street. She couldn't find her bifocals and told me to read the letter to her. I sat opposite her at the kitchen table, my legs entwining a chrome chair leg. After I finished, I was instructed to write back, and I copied down the letter just as my grandmother dictated it.

"Now read it," she said. She lowered her coffee can and wiped the sides of her mouth with her apron.

With all the energy of a toy robot running on low batteries, I read: "Dear _____. How are you? Fine, I hope . . ."

When I was done, my grandmother took the letter from me and looked at it as if she didn't recognize the stationery. I watched warily as she tried to read the letter, squinting.

"Where's that part about 'staying in our prayers'?" she wanted to know. "I can't see this!"

Frustrated, she handed the letter back to me. "Where does it say the part about 'being in our prayers'?"

I had reverted back to direct dictation, no writerly flourishes, no grand salutations. The straight and narrow, that was the road I was taking from now on with her. I'd save my creativity for my own projects.

"You didn't say that," I told her.

"Well," my grandmother said, sending me a rare, slight smile. "Put that in there. That was something nice to say. You should keep that."

seven

SAY SOMETHING

I had grown to love California, but, in the back of my mind, I always assumed that we Lazards would return to St. Louis. Nothing I had experienced made that an unreasonable assumption. Still, without realizing it, I was becoming a Californian, adapting to its mild weather, learning its complicated history, adopting its customs, its slang, and its games.

I joined St. Dominic's girls' kickball team during fifth grade, playing catcher. Our team played all the other fifth-graders in San Francisco's Catholic schools. With Veronica Henderson standing a head taller than the rest of us and serving as our star kicker, we vanquished all the other teams to win the 1969 Catholic Youth Organization (CYO) kickball championship. It was my first sports victory. My first sports trophy. I felt emboldened, hopeful, finally connected to a school experience in a positive way. My mother was proud of me and placed the small trophy—a golden woman with flowing hair and dressed in a flowing gown mounted on a wooden platform—on the dresser of our shared bedroom, a place of honor. I was finally glad that I hadn't skipped fifth grade.

I was looking forward to sixth grade and felt confident and finally connected enough that I decided to run for class officer. With the kickball victory, I had proof that I had contributed to something that had a positive outcome. As sixth-graders we would be the leaders of the school, and I looked forward to that, since in my family I was always the baby, without a voice or power. But, unfortunately, too few people knew me. I didn't win the election. Popularity was for those kids on the other side of Geary—those kids who were neighbors of other kids, whose parents knew each other and worked together and went to the same churches. Or maybe I just didn't campaign hard enough.

Mrs. Velasquez gave us "losers" (that is what she called us!) money to go to the corner store on Pine and Fillmore and buy treats for the victors. Salt in the wounds.

School politics may not have been in my future, but there was still the library, as quietly accepting and steadfast as ever. MaDear and I had settled into a nice routine. She taught me how to pin-curl and style her long hair. We painted each other's nails. I lolled around the house those first few weeks of summer, playing with Pepe. I experimented with the chemistry set Sarah had bought me, dreaming I'd become a chemist, though I didn't really understand what chemists did. My only notion of chemistry was based on mad scientist movies like *Frankenstein*. All scientific experiments were halted, though, after I spilled a potion and discolored Mam'Ella's living room rug. Bored blind, I then tried to teach myself to write left-handed (just in case I lost my right arm in a freak accident; you never know what could happen). I also spent a lot of time watching AAU track and field competitions, hoping one day to become a track star.

Mam'Ella bought an enormous hi-fi console that summer, which provided the best distraction. It was about six feet long and had a dark walnut veneer and burgundy crushed-velvet panels behind faux wood scrollwork, easily the fanciest thing in our house. The hi-fi came with a free Kinks album, but we would have none of that. Mam'Ella blasted Mahalia Jackson and Reverend James Cleveland albums while she cleaned on Saturday afternoons and before heading off to church on Sunday mornings. And when she was in a really good mood she'd play James Brown's *Live at the Apollo*.

My cousin Ed brought over the Temptations' *Psychedelic Shack* and *Cloud Nine* albums. Playing Stevie Wonder's latest, he asked me to transcribe the lyrics to "My Cherie Amour" with all the "la-la-la-la"s so he could present them to some girl he was infatuated with. MaDear and I listened to the new records whenever we had the chance. There was some risk of the Tempts' "You Make Your Own Heaven and Hell Right Here on Earth" supplanting her favorite Otis Redding song in my mother's heart, but Otis, dead then for three years, remained her sentimental favorite. His "(Sittin' on) The Dock of the Bay" was the big hit the year we arrived in San Francisco, and for many in my family it was the song they would always identify as my mother's.

Inspired by all this music, I tried my hand at writing a play based on the *Cloud Nine* album, stringing all the songs together into a narrative. I was still trying to become a writer, trying to figure out how it was done. But on the rare occasions Mam'Ella's usher board members would come to the house and, invariably, ask me what I wanted to be when I grew up, I never said "a writer," fearing they would have the same disapproving reaction as my grandmother had. I'd keep my dreams to myself, thank you very much. I simply responded, "I don't know," careful not to shrug my shoulders. Old ladies hate that.

Together MaDear and I drifted between our house and the board and care home that my grandmother operated across Pine Street. Mam'Ella now took care of adults. At the home, we'd watch Giants baseball with the elaborately coiffed Mrs. Perry, all dolled up for a suitor who never showed. Red lips, gaudy costume jewelry, long painted nails, and a mouthful of gleaming, ill-fitting false teeth. She was a good companion for my mother, who was as plain as a paper bag. As MaDear would say, they "got along swell." Giants baseball never captured my mother's heart like our hometown St. Louis Cardinals had, but she made do. Baseball was still her game despite her favorite player, Curt Flood, being out for the season. Together Mrs. Perry and MaDear smoked cigarettes like nobody's business and chatted about the ballplayers and the weather while, around them, the other six residents of the home paced and mumbled and twitched. I was drawn into the activity there, expected to make coffee, parcel out medications, and mop floors after the residents' accidents. At least Mrs. Perry was able to hold a conversation.

When we got fed up with our routines, my mother and I jumped at the chance to head over to Oakland to spend some time with my Aunt Ruby and her kids, but I didn't especially like being there. Aunt Ruby's house was often loud and chaotic. Her teenaged children battled their drunken stepfather like he was a kid on the playground, so we didn't stay long.

Uncle Shirley took us fishing in rural Tracy one weekend and we stayed in a cabin. I hooked worms on my mother's line because she loved fishing but was terrified of worms. We all listened to Aretha Franklin and Johnnie Taylor songs on Uncle Shirley's eight-track player and ate saltines and salami and drank syrupy-sweet red Kool-Aid and swatted the biggest flies I'd ever seen. It was a departure from the routine, and I wanted more.

Aunt Katie's house was as beautiful and orderly as Aunt Ruby's was disruptive and messy. Katie lived in a modern four-bedroom California ranch–style house on 91st Avenue in East Oakland. It had wall-to-wall carpeting, an intercom system, an electric oven and range, and a sliding glass door that led to a neatly manicured grassy backyard. Fancy. She was married to a plumber who drove a new Cadillac. Of all my cousins, her five children were the most well-dressed, well-fed, and securely housed. Like her mother, Aunt Katie was enterprising. Unlike *my* mother, she was a strong presence: ambitious, outspoken, and independent. She knew what she wanted and knew how to get it.

What You Don't Know Will Make a Whole New World

Katie invested in a grocery store on 16th Street in West Oakland, not far from Uncle Shirley's house. She taught Donna and me to work the counter, to count out customers' change, and to operate the slush machine and meat slicer. My favorite job was cutting meat. In those days people would come and order lunch meat by the pound. "I'll take a half pound of bologna," they'd say, and I'd grab the log of bologna, place it carefully on the metal tray, switch on the slicer, and get to work. I was so proud of myself! It was my first job, unpaid but no less rewarding. Of course, at age eleven, most kids don't know anything about economics, about supply and demand or profit margins. Aunt Katie came back from an errand one afternoon, having left Donna and me to tend the store for a while, and found that the bologna log, which she'd assumed would last for several days, was nearly gone. I was cutting the slices too thick. Between Donna at the slush machine and me at the meat counter, she'd be bankrupt soon!

I'd turned eleven while at her house, and I don't remember much about the day except telling my cousin Donna early in the evening that I was now eleven, to which she replied, "Why didn't you say something? We would've made you a cake."

I had been in California for two years at that point and had assumed that the adults in my extended family would know my birthday, just as my parents had, but it seemed I was still a stranger, that they didn't know anything about me unless I told them.

Back on Pine Street, I was missing Sarah, who had returned to Chicago, her California dreams of becoming a nurse unrealized. My browsing became more aimless without her recommendations. I was a little lost in the library. I wandered the neighborhood with Pepe, trying in vain to train him.

One day Mam'Ella told me about a CYO day camp that I could attend. I jumped at the chance. I hadn't been to camp since my days at St. Vincent's. At the end of the two weeks, I learned, we'd have a long sleepover weekend in Mill Valley, in Marin County. Yay!

On the final Thursday of the camp, I packed early for the sleepover. Instead of coming home, we kids would head out directly from St. Dominic's to Mill Valley. The last time I was at camp, we'd slept in bunks in a mosquito-plagued wooden cabin, but this year we would be in tents. Mam'Ella had borrowed a sleeping bag for me. Being from a family obsessed with cowboy movies, I found the whole idea of sleeping outside, under the stars, thrilling. That morning before camp, with my knapsack on my back and my sleeping bag in my arms, I went into the bedroom to tell my mother goodbye. But before I could lean down for a hug, the phone rang. I answered it.

It was my father's oldest daughter, Mary, who called us occasionally to check in. That morning she asked her usual questions: "How is Lavurn?" "What is Albert up to?" "How are you doing in school?" I told her about my grades (perfect!) and the kickball tournament as I proudly eyed my trophy. I didn't tell her about the election loss.

She was quiet for a moment. I figured she just wasn't that interested in kickball. Then she said, "Daddy died." I cleared my throat.

A moment later, Mary added, "Do you want me to tell Lavurn?"

"When?" For some reason, the date was as important to me as the fact.

"Sunday."

I looked at the small paper calendar from the local funeral home that sat on our dresser. Sunday was August 2, 1970.

"I'll tell her," I said. I didn't know what else to say or how to feel.

"Well," Mary said, trying to bring cheer into her voice. "You be good. Okay?"

"Okay. Bye."

As I slowly placed the phone in its cradle, my mother said, "Your daddy's dead, ain't he?"

I nodded. "Yeah." I wondered how she could know that. "Do you want me to stay?"

"No. Go, and have a good time."

Reluctantly I left her and, within a half hour, I was sitting dumbfounded among a busload of giggling boys and girls, headed to Marin County. My mind was not on archery or swimming or nature hikes or the silly call-and-response camp songs. I was thinking about St. Louis and wondering if I'd ever get back there. And if I did, where would I live without my father there? My mother couldn't work, so she couldn't provide for us. And our moving in with any of my much older half-siblings, who had families of their own, was never a viable option—our time at St. Vincent's had proved that. I wondered about my brother Albert, living away from all of us for the first time. Had Mary called him, too? How had he responded? The possibility of us staying in California forever had never crossed my mind, but now I suddenly felt like I was on a straight path, with no forks in the road. St. Louis was thrown abruptly into the past.

Lying in my sleeping bag under the stars that first night at camp, I wondered if Mr. Bear had died alone, wondered what ailment had struck him, wondered what his last thoughts were, if he had cried out in agony or simply drifted off. I hadn't thought to ask Mary all this. Then all the things I'd meant to ask the old man came to me in a rush: his father's name, the school he attended in New Orleans, how he and my mother met, what it was like to cook for the railroads, if he had a middle name. I wondered for the first time in a long time what might have happened to all of our things back at the old place on Franklin Avenue—our clothes, our furniture, the pots and pans my parents dutifully filled with food, the attic full of ancient toys that had once belonged to his older children. What had become of my father's collection of buffalo nickels, to my rocking horse, to the big galvanized tubs we once bathed in? I wondered where my brother Sam would land the next time his wife threw him out of the house. Under whose window would my brother Henry yell up to for "a few dollars"?

I didn't cry. I was too busy pondering the possibilities.

Lacking the language to describe my fears about what lay ahead for us, I felt a disorienting confusion. I didn't know Jack Lazard well enough to mourn him, I realized. That was a big pill to swallow. We were supposed to love our parents and mourn the dead. But what did mourning call for? Over the course of that long weekend among the redwoods, I realized that I had stopped missing him even before we'd left St. Vincent's. Though my father had been a steady presence in my early life, he never seemed to me essential. It was my mother who I had always pined for when we were separated, my mother who I cried for when I was hurt. While we were at St. Vincent's, Mr. Bear only came to visit us one time, and that was while we were away at camp. Though it was blazing hot, the old man had arrived in a full suit, dabbing his forehead with his big cotton handkerchief like Satchmo. I showed him the various crafts I had made and the tadpoles I had collected in a jar. I don't recall what we talked about, though I'm sure I asked him about MaDear.

When it came time for him to leave, I'd held on to him for dear life, begging him to take me back home—back home to what I was used to, to where I was "normal," to my mother. He had to get Albert to peel my hands off him so he could get back into the cab.

Now among all the calming, bucolic beauty of Mill Valley, I felt guilty because I could not cry, though I felt I should. A lost life deserves tears, doesn't it? It was the old man, after all, who had kept us alive on his meager pension by cooking us pots of gumbo on our birthdays and mackerel croquettes every week, observing the Catholic no-meat Fridays. On Sunday mornings he'd read me the funny pages—*Prince Valiant*, *Beetle Bailey*, and *Blondie*. He sometimes muttered in intriguing foreign languages we didn't understand.

"*Ándale!*" he would call to hurry us out of the house so we would be on time for church. "*Ándale!*"

Now I whispered the word to myself. *Ándale!* Come on! A word that he gave me.

⸻

"My father died," I blurted out to a young camp counselor the next afternoon.

She blinked several times and gulped. "Uh. Oh. I'm sorry."

"Why are you sorry?" I asked.

She had no answer and soon walked away from me as though I had passed gas. Her exit made me feel as though I shouldn't say anything else about it. Maybe, I thought, death isn't something kids are supposed to talk about. In my family, we children were always being told to stay out of grown folks' business. But this death seemed absolutely my business. Still, I didn't tell anyone else. I wondered about my mother and how she was handling the news. I wished I was home with her. I wasn't having fun, not even a little bit.

The only thing that eased my mind that long weekend was remembering that my mother was experiencing a long stretch of good health. For a full year, and possibly for the first time in her adult life, my mother, who had been plagued by grand mal epileptic seizures since she was nineteen, had not experienced a single seizure! It was the closest I'd ever come to witnessing a miracle. I felt she was finally safe. Home free. Maybe there was something magical about Pine Street. But then, Mr. Bear died.

Days later, the kids on the bus—tan, mosquito-bitten, and giggly—sang another round of goofy camp songs (many of them strangely involving Jesus, the devil, or a kookaburra) all the way back to San Francisco. They had worked themselves into an ear-piercing frenzy by the time the bus pulled up to St. Dominic's School. A part of me wanted to join in and be raucous and uninhibited, something that wasn't tolerated in my grandmother's house, but I didn't have the energy. I was preoccupied with pondering next steps, with the impending, unwelcome "new." I remember thinking, "I'm almost an orphan," and wondered what that role would require of me.

When I entered the house on Pine Street, I set my knapsack and borrowed sleeping bag down in the front hallway.

"I'm back!" I called out.

Mam'Ella rushed toward me. Before I could register her mood, she was on me, swinging a belt. Left, right, left across my shoulders and my back. Tearing away at my bare legs. What had I done? Had I left the stove on? Had I accidentally kicked over her slop jar and left a mess when I'd run out days ago? Had I forgotten to give my mother her medicine the morning I'd left? Had she been struggling with seizures the whole time I was gone?

"What did I do?" I asked, reaching for the belt, reaching for her wrist to stop her, once again falling into that violent herky-jerky dance. By eleven I was as tall as Mam'Ella and finally able to defend myself somewhat.

Out of breath, Mam'Ella stepped back.

"Why didn't you tell me your father died?" She breathed heavily and leaned on the hi-fi cabinet.

"I told MaDear." I figured my mother, if she had wanted to, would tell *her* mother.

"You shoulda told *me*!" she barked.

"Why?"

I'd always felt Mam'Ella didn't like my old man, as she had made no effort to reunite us, to communicate with him. Though, at her direction, I had written to family in St. Louis a few times, I had written no letters to him on her behalf.

Steaming, she turned and walked away from me, tossing the belt on the couch. I followed her into the kitchen, where I found my mother at the table nursing a cup of coffee and a few slices of toast. Silent.

I was silent, too, waiting for an explanation.

"If you'd told me, I coulda sent you and Albert out there to the funeral. Now you won't get nothing! Nothing what's coming to you!"

Is that what this was about? Money?! What money does she think he had? And how were we supposed to get it?

"You coulda got something!"

"We can still go back," I offered. At that moment, as welts rose on my legs, that seemed the best idea in the world. Go and don't come back to California at all.

"It's too late now."

She went on to say something about Social Security and pensions, but I didn't understand any of that, so I tuned out. I had no concept of us being poor in St. Louis—not in any specific, demoralizing way—or of my father having any money worth coveting. But we had lived in a cold-water flat above a store. Our toilet was out on the porch, for Chrissake! What did my grandmother want with that? To Ella Baskin, we—MaDear, Albert, and I—were a commodity. Not cherished relations, but a source of income like her foster children, who, by that summer, had all been moved to other homes. It was around this time that I started to understand the estrangement my mother felt from her mother. I was starting to recognize it in myself.

Some days later, I had been out in the sliver of backyard with the dog when I decided to go in and sit on the sun porch for a while to read. When I got up to the door leading to the kitchen, I found it was locked. I tapped on the door. My grandmother came into the kitchen, humming along with something on the hi-fi. She was busily cooking.

"I want to come in," I said through the multi-paned door.

She glanced at me but made no move toward the door.

I knocked again.

She ignored me and carried on as if I was invisible. I yanked at the doorknob and knocked louder, hoping my mother would hear me and come to let me in. Pepe barked. He wanted in, too. I felt myself getting warmer as I knocked and twisted the knob. My heart began to pound.

"Please, let me in. Mam'Ella, please."

She had once done the same thing on Cole Street. A girl whose name I've long forgotten, the bully of the neighborhood, declared she wanted to fight me and had announced to the other girls with assurance that she would beat me. I had no doubt about that. The other kids oohed and aahed at the prospect of witnessing an unprovoked fight. I was the new kid on the block, untried and untested, but I had no beef with this girl. I didn't want to fight her. I didn't want to fight anyone. A day or so after the announcement, the girl appeared on our block ready to rumble.

I ran up the stairs to shelter inside until the girl cooled off or disappeared, but I found the door locked. I called for my grandmother to let me in, for anyone to let me in. I heard Mam'Ella come down the stairs to the door. She pulled the curtain aside to see who was at the door.

Through the door I told her what was happening. She seemed to listen. She looked beyond me at the cluster of girls gathered on the sidewalk. Then she let the curtain fall back into place and, as she climbed the stairs, told me to stay out there and fight.

It was that memory that sparked the rage I felt two years later on that sun porch. I turned away from the door, but instead of returning to my seat, to my book and the story it had pulled me into, to the dog that stood patiently nearby, I threw my left fist into the glass pane nearest the doorknob. I reached through the jagged window, careful not to cut myself, and unlocked the door myself.

Mam'Ella stood stock-still. Hell, even I was stunned at the anger that had flared up in me. It was like nothing I had experienced before. It rattled me. I expected Mam'Ella to come after me with the wooden spatula in her hand, but she just stared. I stared back—another challenge to her authority. I didn't know whether to sweep up the broken glass, go back outside, or go to my room. What do you do after you've done something so unexpectedly defiant and violent? What do you say to someone who ignores you?

Mam'Ella and I were at war, plain and simple.

eight
EAST BAY BOUND

That month, our family picked up stakes again and moved to Oakland to join the rest of the Baskin clan. My grandmother, MaDear, Albert, and I moved to a two-story white house on Birch Street just off 98th Avenue. Compared with the house on Pine Street, this house seemed like paradise, with its small but sunny rooms and no neighboring houses crowding us in. It had a large backyard filled with fruit trees—lemon, plum, loquat, apricot, and fig. My mother and her Aunt Mariah (Aunt Ri, we all called her) preserved fruits downstairs in the large workshop behind the garage. Birch Street was a real neighborhood, with kids in nearly every house. Across the street at Elmhurst Junior High we had a huge, grassy field to play in, racing, chasing each other in games of tag, declaring water balloon fights. I made friends quickly and there were no bullies in sight. Our dog Pepe, who had lost an eye but survived a hit-and-run on merciless Pine Street in San Francisco, was much grumpier with his compromised eyesight, but he loved the room he had to safely roam and all the attention the neighborhood kids paid him.

The women in the family were always around at that time. It wasn't long after our move to Birch Street that Mam'Ella took to her bed. She no longer managed her board and care home. There was no more cooking. No more slow strolls to the laundromat. No more bus rides to church with her. The only lively activity in the house was when my Uncle Melvin came over and watched TV with us. Our favorite show to watch together was the *Wide World of Sports*, with Howard Cosell and Jim McKay. I loved the track and field events. Uncle Melvin preferred boxing. Muhammad Ali was climbing back to the top of the fight game, and Uncle Melvin loved watching him give it to Joe Frazier and any other contender. Ali regaining his crown as heavyweight champ meant more to Uncle Melvin than just a sports victory. Ali had stood up to the US government by refusing to be sent to Vietnam to fight. It had cost him prime earning and boxing years, but his integrity was intact. No Viet Cong ever called him nigger. Uncle Melvin, a Korean War vet, respected that. And I respected it, too, though I thought it was a bold move. An individual taking on the whole government seemed monumental, a David vs. Goliath story if ever there was one. But it taught me to recognize what fight is mine and what fight belongs to someone else.

One afternoon Albert and I were in the backyard picking and eating plums when we heard a thud inside. Being well trained to respond to our mother's sudden seizures, we bounded up the back stairs to the kitchen. Instead of finding MaDear laid out, writing on the floor, we found her tussling with Aunt Ri, throwing punches like Ali. Aunt Ri was giving as good as she got. Albert burst into laughter at this spectacle but managed to separate them. Albert guided our mother into the bedroom we shared. Frozen, I couldn't even guess what might have prompted this brawl.

I would find out a little while later that the two had gotten into it over Mam'Ella's diet. Aunt Ri was cooking as she always had, with grease from the coffee can kept on the stove, and my mother had taken issue with it. No one had explained to me what was going on with Mam'Ella, and I think I was too scared to ask. I was still feeling resentful about her reaction to my father's death. I hadn't said much to her and generally tried to steer clear of her. After the fight in the kitchen, I looked down the hall into Mam'Ella's bedroom where she lay, small and frail, her high cheekbones now even more prominent. There was no "Cut out that noise!" shouted from her room. No more Mahalia Jackson or Reverend Ike blaring through the house on weekend mornings. She no longer gave me errands to run or chores to do. There were no more letters to write. There was no longer a coffee can of tobacco juice to empty. I was called into her room only a few times during our first weeks on Birch Street, but only to deliver her glasses of water.

It seemed as quickly as we had moved in, I was enrolled at Highland Elementary, way over on 85th Avenue and A Street, instead of at

E. Morris Cox, a mere two blocks away. The decision didn't make sense until, less than a month after my move to Oakland, I was sent to live on 91st Avenue with Aunt Katie, her five kids, and her husband. New again.

At the same time, Albert was dispatched to Uncle Shirley's house in West Oakland, where he was enrolled at McClymonds High School. Living with five small boys under the age of seven must have been a challenge for him. But having an able-bodied male figure to answer to must've been even harder for Albert, who, given our father's old age, had had no strong male authority for most of his life. Uncle Shirley expected kids to behave and stay on the right track, and Albert, as always, was determined to live life on his own terms.

My grandmother Ella Baskin died in March 1971. The cause was stomach cancer. In the coming years I would realize just how much this short, ambitious, religious woman had held our family together. Maybe it was her faith and all that praying. Maybe it was the shame of the doghouse plaque that kept people in line. In her absence, big holiday dinners that used to draw everyone together fell slowly by the wayside. Conflicts between family members festered. Cousins got involved in drugs and criminal activity. A number of them were incarcerated. Mam'Ella wouldn't have stood for any of that.

Aunt Katie set up a little house on 98th Avenue near A Street to continue caring for some of the people Mam'Ella had been responsible for in San Francisco. Unfortunately, the wonderfully ornate Mrs. Perry didn't migrate across the bay with them. With

Albert and I farmed out to different relatives, MaDear moved in with Aunt Ri, who lived around the corner from this new board and care home.

I found my first months in Oakland unsettling. Once again my family was separated, and that caused me some anxiety. But at least this time I knew how to get to everyone. I missed San Francisco, not only for its Victorian charm but for my opportunity to roam my neighborhood alone, to spend quiet time in the public library, day-dreaming, imagining myself on wild adventures. I had taken it all for granted. Oakland was an altogether different scene. I had nothing close to privacy, which, even as a kid, I sometimes craved. In those early days in Oakland I had little relationship with the library; the stimulation now was social, not literary. Among my cousins, I was learning how to be a kid, learning to while away time in play and idle chatter and TV shows—*Star Trek* reruns, *The Brady Bunch*, or *Room* 222—chosen by consensus. The library took a withering insignificance in the face of so much distraction.

In our Elmhurst neighborhood, kids poured out of most houses. We played in the streets, in people's backyards, in driveways, in schoolyards. Kids knew how to play back then, with or without store-bought toys. We raced each other, skated, and held jump rope competitions. We ran laughing whenever a rogue dog got loose and came after us. We rode three to a bike, with one kid pumping furi-ously while another kid sat behind on the banana seat and a third sat wedged in between the handlebars. We raided the fruit trees that grew in abundance in our neighborhood, drawing their owners outside with brooms, with old (and unloaded, we hoped) rifles, and threats to rat us out to our parents. We found fun everywhere. The assumption, yielded far too early in our lives, was that life was a gas!

But none of this fun came naturally to me. It took a while before I let go of the impulse to head inside to visit my mother, make her a cup of coffee, or fry up a pan of potatoes and onions. My grandmother's illness and death left a big void in my daily routine, and I found it challenging to fill. There were enough adults around now for me to lay down the responsibilities that had ruled my life over in San Francisco. It was my turn to be a kid. But I felt at loose ends with my peers, like when you struggle to find the perfect moment to jump into the double-dutch ropes to avoid getting smacked in the face. Kids didn't talk about much of anything important, but I didn't fall naturally into their idle name-calling and gentle and not-so-gentle teasing.

"Yo mama so ugly she can make a mirror crack."

"Well, well . . . yo mama so fat she got her own zip code."

My cousins—Donna, Jackie, and their older brother Kenny—provided me with entry into this world, but even though I loved watching their play, their socializing, I felt apart, different in experience and attitude. I wasn't prone to superstitions; I didn't believe, for instance, that I would break my mother's back if I stepped on a crack in the sidewalk. I kept quiet to fortify myself against any taunts, especially the ones about mamas, and I had to negotiate who to trust and who to steer clear of. I wasn't big on the frivolity that is such a part of any normal childhood, but I longed to be, if not popular, at least accepted, not an outlier.

Reluctantly I learned that childhood was not supposed to be a solitary endeavor, a camp that you could roll into and out of. I was part of a larger, interconnected unit. A family. My free-range childhood was basically over. I was accountable. I was a cousin, and an older cousin at that, and was accountable to my aunt and my cousins in a way that I had never been before. If one of the younger cousins fell, did something wrong, put themselves in jeopardy in some way, I would be scolded.

"Why'd you let them do that?" I'd be asked.

I'd never considered myself an authority figure. Never aspired to be one either. Being responsible for my mother and occasionally the patients at my grandmother's board and care home was the responsibility I was accustomed to having. As the youngest in my immediate family, I found this new responsibility for other children a challenge. Kids had minds of their own, and who was I to question that?

It was in these social circles that I started to understand how many types of Black kids there were. There were middle-class kids and working-class kids, kids with only a mom to take care of them, kids who were dirt poor. Our neighborhood held multitudes. I got to tour all these different realities whenever Donna and I accompanied Kenny on his paper route, three to a three-speed bike. Kenny loved his bike. It gave him the wide-ranging freedom that boys were allowed. Having the means and motivation to stray farther away from the homestead, I knew, was an education, a type of currency that all too often girls were denied.

One day Aunt Katie sent Donna and me to Food King, the big grocery store on East 14th Street, to pick up something she needed for our dinner. It was far enough away that we were allowed to take Kenny's bike. When we got there, Donna said to me, "Watch the bike," and headed inside. I lazily circled the parking lot a few times, stopping at the side door each time to see if Donna had come out. Then I got the bright idea to steal a Hostess Brownie. I had seen other kids steal things and run gleefully away with their loot. It seemed like such a lark. I rolled the bike back and forth, pondering my chances. The cupcake aisle was only a few yards away. I got off the bike and lingered at the door, waiting for Donna, waiting for my chance. Then I decided to go for it. But just as soon as I got a grasp on the brownie and turned toward the door, one of the store clerks got a grip on the collar of my dress. By the time my scolding was over and I was released, Donna and I stepped outside to discover that Kenny's beloved bike had been stolen. Walking back home to 91st Avenue was the longest, most dreaded walk I had ever taken—like those slow walks to the electric chair the gangsters take in those old James Cagney movies. Needless to say, Aunt Katie tore into me. And I deserved it. A life of crime was not for me. I was pretty bad at being bad.

Our family clustered close together always. Uncle Shirley and his family moved around the corner on B Street, and Aunt Noonie, my mother's youngest sibling, lived with her family a few blocks away on C Street. So it was never hard to get us together. One day Noonie's girls—Yvette, Debbie, and Kat—and cousin Marie's toddler, Theresa, came over to play. Eventually we ended up back inside, running through the house, making a circuit through Aunt Katie's living room, the hallway, the rumpus room, and into the other hallway, giggling, laughing, making sure not to run over the little ones. At one point it wasn't clear who was chasing who, but we kept it going. I was making another circuit through the living room, running behind everyone else, when I was caught from behind. It felt like it was someone my height, but it wasn't Donna, the only other playmate my height. A hairy yellow arm wrapped tight around my chest. It was the plumber, Aunt Katie's husband. As I tried to pull away, he held me tighter and dug his free left hand into my shorts, his thick fingers probing. I didn't know what he was doing, or why he was doing it. I just knew it felt wrong. And I wondered if he had been catching everyone and ensnaring them in this way. Should I holler out? *Could* I holler out? What would I say, and who would I call? Aunt Katie wasn't at home. I was frozen. Dumbfounded. As he grabbed at my budding breasts and squeezed hard, something shifted in my brain and I began to struggle to free myself. Then he pushed me away. I was too afraid to look back at him, afraid if I made eye contact he would come after me again. I just ran outside, suddenly in no mood for fun and games.

nine

THE FIRST LAW OF NATURE

Sometime during my seventh-grade year, Aunt Katie and her family moved from 91st Avenue into a much more modest brown-shingled house on C Street, across the street from Aunt Noonie. My mother and I moved with them, sharing a back room that had been converted into a bedroom. Now that Mam'Ella was gone, the responsibility for my nuclear family fell to Aunt Katie. Her marriage to the plumber had ended or was ending—I don't remember the exact timeline—so it was just us kids and the two sisters.

One day Katie drove up to the house in a camper and announced that she was taking Donna and Jackie to Disneyland. On impulse, I begged to go along. The summer had me bored. I thought roaming around in a cool vehicle that you could sleep in would be an amazing adventure. I had never been on a vacation before. Besides, I didn't want Donna and Jackie, my ambassadors to childhood activities, to leave me behind to navigate a new crop of kids on my own. I begged MaDear to let me go. She said she'd consent only if it was okay with Katie. I turned my pleas to my aunt, promising that I'd be good and wouldn't take up too much space. We had had our run-ins about my sassy mouth, but I was willing to conform to any behavior codes in order to go.

But I didn't know when I was doing all that begging that the plumber was coming along on the trip. Once I found out, it seemed too late to decline the opportunity. I figured that, in such close quarters, I'd surely be safe from this man and his roaming hands. But that was wishful thinking. Whenever anyone's back was turned, the plumber grabbed at my chest, poked his finger at my crotch, drove his hands down my pants. I never saw him treat my cousins this way. After Disneyland—which I retained no memory of—we headed to his sister's place in Reno. Donna and Jackie were given the spare bedroom to sleep in, and despite the fact that Donna and I had slept in the same twin bed for the better part of the previous year, I was directed to the couch along the wall that separated the living room from the kitchen.

I couldn't get to sleep because of all the talking and laughing the adults were doing in the kitchen. They were up late, drinking, playing cards, and gossiping. I tossed and turned for most of the evening and was just about to drift off to sleep when I felt a hand moving up my leg. I knew whose hand it was, but I could not believe he'd be so bold. Not with Aunt Katie just a few feet away. Frozen, I couldn't believe he had so little regard for me.

Ever since that first encounter, I had lurked around the edges of every room he might be in. Shrinking. Trying not to be seen. That night, I don't know if it was fear I felt so much as a sickening vulnerability. I didn't want to feel like that anymore. Silently I pushed his hand aside, threw the covers back. I marched into the kitchen, head down, saying nothing to Aunt Katie and the other women. I opened a kitchen drawer and pulled out a butcher knife. I returned to the living room and pointed the knife at him. Of course, I had no idea how to fight or to wield a knife. I was just using it as a shield, a definitive way to say, "I'm not taking this anymore."

I can't recall how long I held the knife, nor do I remember how far away from him I stood with it, or if he made a move to take it from me. I just knew I wasn't letting it go. And if it wasn't bad enough that her husband was putting his hands on me, it hurt to know that my Aunt Katie, who a few years earlier had been my champion with Mrs. Wyke, never got up to see what I was doing with the knife. I couldn't sort out why he came after *me*, and I didn't have language to talk to her about her husband's actions, so I said nothing. I was young enough, naive enough, to think that, even if I could piece together the words to describe what he was doing to me, what he made me feel when he touched me, I'd get into trouble. My living situation was precarious enough; I didn't want to jeopardize it. I hadn't learned how to talk about my feelings. Anyway, I didn't think Aunt Katie would believe me. So, I opted for the knife.

When I woke up the next morning the knife was gone—back in its place, I assumed, in the kitchen drawer.

Children who sit on the fringes of families are vulnerable to predators. I didn't know it then, but I would come to realize that sad fact years later. The neglected, disrespected, unwanted are the collateral in families, the fodder that predators hope to and all too often find. There was something about my role in my family that communicated to the plumber that I was prey.

Albert always said, "Self-preservation is the first law of nature." And, instinctively, on some cellular level, I now understood that to be true. I owned nothing at the time but my body, and I felt I had to protect it. Being a preteen girl was and, sadly, remains a perilous enterprise. It's the age when your body begins to betray your innocence and sends signals to boys and men that you want something that you *don't* want and aren't ready to handle emotionally or physically. The groping begins early and happens often. It tells girls that their bodies are public property, that the vessels they carry around are not theirs and can be easily handled, ridiculed, and abused. Just as your body is reaching new levels of physical maturity, you lose what little sovereignty you have over it. It's little wonder that girls' confidence plummets around this age.

Before my aunt's husband's violation, there was a boy in my fifth-grade class at St. Dominic's School who'd pin me against the wall on the staircase and grab at my budding breasts or pull up my school uniform to expose my underwear. What I found galling was not only the fact that he wanted to but that he felt he had the right to touch me without my permission. Our culture shrugs and tells us "boys will be boys," and that was supposed to justify their predatory behavior. I never saw girls grabbing boys by the crotch and laughing with their friends about it. Boys were given freedom to move through spaces, welcomed or not, grabbing everything that caught their eye. To become, if they wanted to, aggressors. Girls, on the other hand, were taught to be quiet and acquiesce, always operating under the threat of someone's disapproval. I never could stomach that. I hated feeling frozen, mute.

ten

SHAME

Elmhurst Junior High School offered me another opportunity to remake myself. But the reconstruction would not be easy. I would officially become Dorothy Lazard, not Ann Lazard, as I had been known in elementary school. It seemed a fitting time to finally use my more mature-sounding first name.

I knew right away that junior high would be a challenge like none I'd faced before. It was thrilling and scary and bewildering all at once, and it demanded that I expand my social horizons. I liked having six classes with six teachers to negotiate each day. I took French, social studies, and art. My English classes forced me to return to writing.

Despite all the feminist cigarette and deodorant ads, and white women singing on variety shows about being a "W-O-M-A-N," girls in the early 1970s were still required to take typing and home economics all three years of junior high—preparation, I assumed, to become useful homemakers and mothers. Mrs. Greenberg, the petite home economics teacher, taught us how to read sewing patterns and use a Singer sewing machine. We sewed smocks and bell-bottoms and reversible vests. We made layer cakes, jam, fruit pies, and, much to our eternal confusion, lamb chops with mint jelly. I didn't know anyone who ever ate lamb chops. And who, we wondered, eats jelly with meat?

My biggest challenge was gym class. At seventh-grade orientation, we girls were told that our families would have to buy us the requisite two-piece gym uniform: blue shorts and a blue short-sleeve, snap-button top. Rumor had it that Elmhurst had once been a girls' reformatory, and with our blue uniforms on, we all looked like inmates. In gym class—required of all students back then—we went through a rotation of gymnastics, softball, volleyball, and hokey folk dances for which we learned to "allemande left with the corner gal." We did general calisthenics accompanied by the booming voice of actor Robert Preston singing "Chicken Fat," which was goofy and fun. The only thing that wasn't fun about gym class was showering.

I had long mastered the mechanics of the shower since that first confusing encounter at St. Vincent's Day Home, but junior high set me back a bit. There were no individual stalls, just open areas with several showerheads lined along the walls, like you'd see in prison movies. We were expected to shower after class in front of complete strangers and even friends, at the very time when we were most self-conscious about our ever-changing bodies. To be scoped out, judged, and mocked by girls who were more physically developed was brutal. I was as thin as a greyhound and was often teased about it. In the shower, I followed the lead of those girls who had learned to contort themselves out of their clothes without showing too much skin. Unhook your bra, slip your arms out of your blouse or dress, pull the bra off through the top of your blouse or the sleeve of your dress, and lay it on the bench near you. Hold a towel clamped under your arms across your chest as you shimmy out of your pants or skirt. Keep your towel wrapped around you until you get to the nearest available showerhead, then find a place to lay the towel so it doesn't get soaked. Hope like hell no one takes it while you're in the shower. Show as little skin as possible and get out of there as fast as you can. In other words, feel ashamed of your body. Waiting till most girls showered meant you'd likely be late for your next class. I envied the girls who could stroll into the showers after a game of softball like they owned the place and saunter back to their lockers, naked as a jaybird, as my mother would say. They had accepted themselves in a way that I had yet to learn.

And let's not even talk about our hair! Protecting one's press-and-curl was its own separate project for us Black girls. Since I was in junior high school now, I was trying to look "decent," grow my short hair out, and wear it in curls. Trying to protect our hair from the steam and water of the shower was an exercise in futility, since few of us had shower caps. And what happened in the shower never stayed in the shower. Teasing was not off-limits in junior high. It seemed compulsory.

For all the shame that lay in that institutional locker room, we had wings to try on in some of our other classes. We were in the early 1970s in the midst of a Black cultural revolution bigger than anything since the Harlem Renaissance of the 1920s. Yet we still carried a lot of shame about our kinky hair and dark skin. When someone called you "black" it was not intended as a compliment. It was enough to cause a fight. We kids had to grow out of our self-loathing. For the first time in my life, though, I had Black teachers— Mr. Simpson for science, Ms. Cremer and Mrs. Posey for art. Mr. Julien taught us French. And they were not simply Black, they were evangelically Black. The graceful and professional ways they carried themselves communicated to us that there was no shame in being Black. They were proud of who they were and where they had come from, and they encouraged us to feel the same. In art class, Mrs. Posey, with her perfectly shaped Afro and gorgeous African tribal jewelry, posted works of Black artists, showing Black bodies regal, stately, and confident. She let us know if what we were creating in class was similar to the works by practicing Black artists. She introduced me to collage, which I would develop a lifelong fascination for, as well as poster art, which made me consider a career in graphic design. Mr. Julien told us about the Francophone diaspora and encouraged my French studies. Like me, he had roots in Louisiana, where many people spoke French. Having a foreign language in your quiver of skills opened up the world, he told us. He taught us how to say the Pledge of Allegiance in French.

"Je promets ma fidélité au drapeau des États-Unis d'Amérique . . ."

I couldn't make out when we'd ever have to recite the pledge— we struggled to recite it in English, much less French—but I liked committing something so exotic to memory. Decades later, I can still recite it.

One day, he assured me, I'd travel the world and speak French when I got there. Still dreaming of an adventurous life, I hoped he was right.

Occasionally the boys and girls would be called together into the gym, and the collapsible wall that usually separated us by gender was pulled back for a special lecture or demonstration. One day, one of the boys' gym teachers, Mr. Chatman—tall, lean, and domino black—came in and stood before us. We didn't know what to expect. Chatman commanded respect; he didn't take any backtalk of any kind from any kid, so we sat in respectful silence. I had watched him break up the biggest, most violent brawls single-handedly, then wheelbarrow the instigators of the fight into the principal's office. Instead of the lecture I expected, however, Mr. Chatman mounted the large trampoline that was set up behind him. He started out slow. Bounce, bounce, bounce. Within seconds, he was vaulting in the air, four feet, six feet, eight feet, arms straight out in front, and then he jack-knifed, then corkscrewed into a twist. Effortlessly he somersaulted, did a double twist, a backflip. He was, quite literally, poetry in motion, all form and focus. We kids were in awe, our eyes following him as he neared the ceiling of the gym. His mastery of the trampoline silenced even the rowdiest characters. Then, just as quietly as he had begun, he slowed down, flipped into a dismount, and landed, standing erect next to the trampoline like a conductor in front of an orchestra. It was his control, his physical self-possession, that I found most alluring. Who knew Old Man Chatman could do such a thing? Who knew Black folks could master this strange apparatus? But Mr. Chatman owned his body in a way that no kid at Elmhurst seemed to. We were just learning what to do with our bodies as they grew taller, thicker, hairier, and smellier.

The social waters of Elmhurst Junior High were choppier than I had expected. There were hundreds of kids and dozens of social cliques to navigate. I didn't see myself as a leader, and I wasn't at all interested in becoming a follower. Emotions swung wildly: Kids could meet and become best friends or they could end the day in a fist fight. Rumors ran wild and cut deep. I skimmed the surface, never fully committing to any one group, reasoning that if you don't get too close, you won't get too hurt. I tried always to float in the comfortable middle of the social pool, not popular but not one of the kids who got bullied regularly. I used humor as my armor, poking fun at myself with a preemptive strike before anyone else could launch a harmful insult. I set up shop comfortably on the edges. School dances? I leaned against the walls, doing all the moves in my head. Whenever a boy would approach, I'd freeze. I'd lie, saying that I didn't want to dance or, simply, rudely, "no." Then I'd be angry at myself for lying, for being too afraid to have someone see me thrash around on the dance floor, ignoring the fact that I could only get better at dancing if, and only if, I danced. The risks felt too great.

In my family, it was my job to walk my mother down C Street toward a board and care home where she'd spend her time until mid-afternoon, when someone else in the family would pick her up and take her home. One morning we were ambling down the street at a snail's pace when my English teacher, Mr. Byrne, pulled up in his sedan to the corner of 98th and C on his way to Elmhurst. He leaned over the passenger seat to roll down the window.

"Good morning, Dorothy. Hello. Is this your mother?"

I paused before answering. "Yes, it is," I said, stepping away from the car.

"Hello, Mrs. Lazard."

My heart fluttered. I had not heard anyone call her that in years. No one ever called her that anymore. She was just "Sis" to her younger siblings or "Aunt Lavurn" to my many cousins. MaDear had no identity in wider society. No job, no social status, no friends, no money that would *give* her a formal identity. She had been some-one's wife, I was reminded. But I didn't really understand what kind of currency that held.

My mother leaned down to look inside the car. "Who is that?"

"It's Mr. Byrne," I said. "My English teacher."

It was the first time I could recall my mother meeting one of my teachers. Instantly self-conscious, I looked at her plain cotton dress, her worn shoes, the coffee stains on her clothes. Why hadn't I asked her to change? Why hadn't it bothered me before?

He asked if we needed a ride anywhere. Though a lift would have been easy, I didn't want to tell him where we were headed. I didn't want to say that my mother needed care during the day, that she had epilepsy. So I declined.

"Well, Dorothy is a good student, Mrs. Lazard."

My mother smiled at Mr. Byrne and placed her hand on the top of the car as she leaned in for a conversation. "Yes," she beamed. Then MaDear added her standard boast: "She's never been sick a day in her life."

I was embarrassed by this non sequitur.

I was to walk MaDear to the house on 100th Avenue, but I didn't want to explain all that to Mr. Byrne. I wouldn't know where to begin even if I tried. So my mother and I feigned like we were normal people, even though we were far from it. She insisted that I take a ride with the nice teacher, assuring me that her stiff-legged, unbalanced gait was stable enough to make it down the long block without assistance. There were no more crosswalks to navigate, but there were several driveways.

"You go on and have a good day. Nice to meet you, Mr. Byrne," she said, nodding her approval of his generous gesture. *I am able,* she seemed to be saying. *I am all right.*

I didn't want to argue with her in front of Mr. Byrne. I never argued with her.

"Okay . . . just a minute," I said to him, confused about what to do.

I wanted him to believe that we *were* capable of regular things. But then I looked down the block, took hold of my mother's hand, and set out walking her toward her destination. When we'd made it to the third or fourth house on the block, MaDear pulled away from me. Her thin, elegant fingers opened and untwined themselves from my hand.

"Go. Go. Go on, now. Don't keep your teacher waiting. I think it's swell he wants to give you a ride."

"Are you sure you're gonna be okay?" I asked. There were several more houses and driveways to pass.

She insisted that she would be fine. "Go on, now."

We looked back at the car idling on the corner. I was half-hoping that Mr. Byrne would drive off and I'd be left to carry out my duties as expected.

Reluctantly, I nodded, took a deep breath, then trotted back to Mr. Byrne.

"Your mom's nice," he said in his cheery voice once I closed the car door and he headed up 98th Avenue.

"Yeah," was all I could manage.

When I got home from school that afternoon, I learned that my mother had fallen on the way to her destination and broken her leg. I was devastated, ashamed of myself, scared for her. Aunt Katie scolded me something awful! And I felt that all of her vitriol was entirely justified. I had failed to protect my mother—my most important job—and I was wrecked.

eleven

VILLAGE LIFE

S arah returned to California and soon announced that she had found a place of her own. I leaped at the chance to move in with her. Ever dutiful to the family, Sarah didn't say no. And she didn't take just me on, but Albert and MaDear, too. The two-bedroom apartment she found was in a village of fourplexes on the dog leg of 99th Avenue, its courtyard shady with mature willow trees. We had a second-floor flat, the smallest place we'd lived in since coming to California, but at least it was ours. Becoming guardian and supporter of all of us was a big responsibility for Sarah. She was still trying to make her way through college after a number of false starts. We lived off of my father's Social Security survivor checks and Sarah's meager salary working at a West Oakland nursery school.

While 91st Avenue was full of kids, 99th Avenue was full of teenagers and young adults who were heavily into partying. The musky aroma of marijuana permeated the village. Pills had also flooded the neighborhood, and occasionally we'd hear of someone ODing on bennies or speed at a house party. The drug use led to some pretty wild behavior—stolen cars, house burglaries, purse snatchings. A local politician's son robbed the Kentucky Fried Chicken on the corner of 99th and East 14th Street so regularly that some adults thought he may as well work there since he showed up so often. All the employees and many neighbors knew the rogue by name.

Albert, true to his nature, was drawn to all the chaos. He approached smoking weed like it was a vocation. After his girlfriend moved to Chicago, he ran up our phone bill so high that

My big brother Albert at nineteen, around the time he left Oakland for Chicago.

we risked having it disconnected. He contributed no financial or household help. He ate the majority of whatever food we had. And he was unapologetic about all of it. Albert was what we'd now call "disregulated." No amount of reasonable talk or familial regard corrected his behavior. Sarah, only five years his senior, held no sway. He didn't respect her. And our mother, who had long ago stopped being a parental influence on him, had no power to change him. Our short time in California had been time enough for me to stop looking at him as a role model. He hadn't been around much to provide me with guidance or protection anyway, even if he had been so inclined. There was something about living among a larger family unit that had segregated us, made us less beholden to one another. I was expected to hang out with the younger girl cousins, and he gravitated toward the older male cousins. At thirteen I was beginning to understand that we were all victims of his whims. If he could get out of something by putting someone else between himself and the punishment, he threw us to the wolves.

One day before we left San Francisco, Albert and I were in the garage of our grandmother's board and care home, and Aunt Katie's station wagon was parked inside. It was unlocked, and that, to Albert, was an irresistible temptation.

"Get in!" he told me.

I did, thinking that he'd only pretend to drive it, twisting the steering wheel like little kids often do. I didn't know if Albert knew how to drive or not. He was sixteen years old. Who would've taught him? With Aunt Katie right upstairs, I was sure he wouldn't be bold enough to start the car. But he did. He put the car in gear and tapped the accelerator, but instead of going forward, the car jerked backward and hit a support beam.

We jumped out of the car to assess the damage. The chrome fender was dented just a little, but it was certainly noticeable. Albert's mind worked fast. He was used to getting in trouble. I, on the other hand, was not. How, I wondered, would he get out of this mess? Suddenly my brain was as thick as summer fog. But Albert had concocted an alibi before I could get my thoughts together.

"Let's say you did it," he offered.

Wait. What? Me? The fog didn't lift.

"Me?!"

"Yeah. You won't get in as much trouble as I will."

I thought that was probably true, but how had I gotten involved in this mess at all? It wasn't my idea to get into the car. I had no interest in driving, or in pissing Aunt Katie off. But I also didn't have a comeback, a defense against this dangerous plan. We played it off like nothing was wrong—until it was time for Aunt Katie to go home. She discovered the damage right away, and Albert and I, back at our house across Pine Street, were called over to the board and care home to explain ourselves.

I was at a loss for words. I didn't want to rat Albert out, although I knew what he did was dumb, but I also didn't want to be held responsible. And I had been there, so I was at least partially culpable. Out of loyalty, out of stultifying fear, I followed Albert's game plan. When Aunt Katie, holding a belt that she could crack like Annie Oakley in a Wild West show, asked what happened to her car, I said I didn't know. It was clear by the look on her face that she didn't believe me as soon as I'd said it, but that didn't save me, because now I was lying. And lying to protect someone who wasn't brave enough to stand up for his own actions! She spared no energy in meting out that punishment. The thing that made it tolerable was that Albert was promised a similar fate, and it would be doled out not by Aunt Katie but by one of our uncles, who would go hard on him. Justice. But just a little.

One of my earliest childhood memories is of Albert being involved in the arguments and the resulting physical altercations between our parents. I didn't always know what specific stresses and incidents started these conflicts, but one common reason was Albert's behavior. He often stole things from local stores, and when our ancient father would demand that he return the items (a Duncan yo-yo, a Batmobile dashboard, any number of things), a fight would ensue—a fight that no one really won. These fights never improved Albert's behavior and usually sent MaDear into a seizure. Or sometimes worse. The first photograph of our mother I remember seeing was an eight-by-ten glossy of her in front of our apartment, holding her stomach while being led into an ambulance, her sundress drenched in blood. I don't remember how old I was or how my parents came to have such a photograph, or if I was even there when this event occurred, but I do clearly recall many fights in which our parents and Albert were wedged in a corner of our kitchen, tearing and tugging and swinging at each other. MaDear was always in the middle, trying to protect her precious boy. Maybe I picked up that message from her: protect Albert, no matter the cost.

I drew inward, toward the only thing I felt I had control over: my mind. I hardly ever went to the library anymore—the dozen blocks to the Elmhurst branch was enough to discourage me—but instead of books I was drawn to the intoxicating, glossy wonderland of magazines. At the pharmacy on the corner of 96th Avenue and

East 14th you could stand and read magazines all afternoon. There I discovered new publications like *Essence*, a magazine exclusively for Black women, and *Entertainment Rap!*, a Black movie magazine filled with celebrity news, film reviews, and interviews. Old standbys like *Jet*, the lurid *Bronze Thrills*, and the upwardly mobile *Ebony* were available, too.

I also hadn't given up on writing. On the contrary, I had grown obsessed with storytelling, and came to realize that everything was a part of or an inspiration for a story. Even more than reading, I liked listening to people talk. I guess that sprang from my love of movies and my early years listening to radio broadcasts with my parents. I wasn't writing much down then, but every waking hour, I imagined a whole parade of characters, doing things that I couldn't do or hadn't done, figuring out life, and being elsewhere.

The television became our family's most treasured possession. People called it the "idiot box" then, but for me it was the story box. I became a student of TV, watching even the moralistic anti-drug tales geared to teens to dissuade us from going down the "wrong path." Since I had to stick close to home, I religiously watched talk shows in the afternoon, toggling back and forth between *The Mike Douglas Show* and *The Merv Griffin Show*, which were inconveniently scheduled at the same time. Merv was more of an entertainer who liked to dish with the celebrities he knew, but Mike, who seemed to me less of an interviewer and more of a friendly facilitator, allowed his celebrity co-hosts to invite guests that *they* wanted to talk with—politicians and athletes and writers.

Talk shows introduced me to people who could draw amazing tales from memory. I marveled at how easily and dramatically people like Orson Welles and Orson Bean, George Kirby and Nipsey Russell could tell stories. There was pacing, details, suspense, puns, and humor in their stories.

On Saturday mornings, before *Soul Train*, I watched old Mickey Rooney and Shirley Temple movies from the 1930s and 1940s, wondering how these simple stories had remained popular over the decades even though the world and our sensibilities had changed so dramatically. The fact that they were even still broadcast told me something about the value of nostalgia in our society. Cowboy movies—still my mother's favorite—had given way to police procedurals like *The Rookies* and *The Streets of San Francisco*, and through them I learned the orthodoxy of episodic television. MaDear had explained to me long ago that if someone is in the opening credits, they'll be back the following week, no matter how roughed-up they got this week. I would come to call this the "Little Joe Cartwright phenomenon." On *Bonanza*, my favorite character, Joe Cartwright, would occasionally get beaten up, bitten by a snake, kidnapped, or suffer some other misfortune, and this would send me into fits of anxiety about him not returning next week. But in those days there was little chance of a starring actor being killed off. My worries were unfounded.

Our little village, with its diverse cast of characters, held a whole world of drama of its own, enough to sustain a respectable soap opera: interracial marriage, teen pregnancy, domestic violence, contrite husbands, vindictive wives, rebellious kids, bullies, best friends, struggling single moms, first loves, and cute, precocious kids.

Accompanying all this activity was the most incredible music, which poured out of front doors, car windows, and barbershops. And that fueled more stories. I had stopped writing down most of them. I couldn't write fast enough. I just had an endless mental script being continuously written and revised in my head, stories filled with interconnecting plotlines and a revolving cast of characters.

The early 1970s was the first best time to be a Black kid in America. In just a few short years, the word "black" had gone from being a slur to being an affirming identifier thanks to James Brown singing "Say It Loud—I'm Black and I'm Proud," the burgeoning Black Arts Movement, and progressive groups like the Black Panthers. We kids, who were tagged with the word "negro" on our birth certificates, now had a word we could claim that acknowledged the current political moment of Black empowerment and self-determination. "Black" became a source of pride. At Elmhurst Junior High, I had Black teachers for the first time in my life. They were young, intelligent, creative, attractive, and committed to making us better, inspired, and, if they could manage it, safe. A fundamental part of making us better was teaching us to love ourselves, something white teachers had never openly encouraged. Their expressions of Black excellence—through art practice, gymnastics, foreign language, appreciation of literature—was the start of a cultural rewiring that would continue through our teen years and young adulthood. We kids ingested that message, completely aware that it was a unique gift, one that our older brothers and sisters and certainly our parents never had in their youth. When Aretha sang Nina Simone's "To Be Young, Gifted and Black," it hit me like a mission statement.

More than at any other time in my life, the music I listened to influenced my impressions of the world. The soul prophet Curtis Mayfield, a more political Marvin Gaye, and Stevie Wonder, with his masterworks *Innervisions* and *Talking Book*, introduced us young people to more mature, socially relevant songs that raised our consciousness. In a decade, Stevie had evolved from a preteen singing "Fingertips" to a grown man performing powerful songs like "Big Brother" and "You Haven't Done Nothin'," sharp commentaries on the sorrowful state of government and race relations in America. We not only enjoyed the music but talked about the music as a significant social document of the times. Liner notes became popular, and we kids copied them down to memorize the words so we could sing along whenever we heard them, at home or on KDIA radio. Record stores were like Mecca. You could go down to West Coast Records on East 14th Street near 73rd Avenue and, even if you didn't have enough money to buy anything, the owner would let you browse LPs and listen to an endless number of records. I discovered reggae, new jazz, and other types of music. Through music I was learning that everyone, not just politicians, had a political voice and the agency to impact society.

What You Don't Know Will Make a Whole New World

We were all advocating for something—civil rights, peace, visibility, love, respect.

After my mother's fall on C Street, I spent a lot of time indoors with her, determined not to let her down again. I vowed to be vigilant. Even if it meant staying in the house more than I wanted to. After her cast was removed, MaDear was instructed to use a walker. Navigating it around our tiny apartment, crashing into things, getting wedged between the couch and the coffee table, really pissed her off. She had enough problems with walking already, and the walker only complicated things. She was frustrated and could fly into fits of rage without warning.

A few days a week I shuttled her between our house and Aunt Ri's little cottage, just a block away on A Street. Despite their brawl on Birch Street when my grandmother was dying, my mother and her aunt got along fine. They were good companions and talked a lot more than my mother and Mam'Ella had.

Aunt Ri was the only old woman I knew who lived alone. It seemed she was quite content with her solo existence. Sometimes she'd call me over to run errands for her, usually to the store. And, like her sister had, Aunt Ri charged me with emptying the rusting coffee can she used as a spittoon. She dipped snuff. Her house was like a museum, full of interesting things—mismatched china, crocheted doilies, and old calendars from funeral homes. Just as you stepped into her house, there was a small table that held a sepia-toned photograph of a beautiful young woman dressed in a smart suit like the ones Barbara Stanwyck wore in the old movies. One day I asked about the photograph.

"Who is she?"

"That's my daughter."

"Does she live in Chicago?"

"No, she don't live anywhere. She's dead."

I was too afraid to ask how she came to die, thinking Aunt Ri would feel like I was being nosy, but after a while she said: "She got hold of that narcotic. That narcotic killed her. She's been dead a long time."

I don't remember if I asked her daughter's name or if I said I was sorry, or even if I felt sorry at the time. But from that day on Aunt Ri never had to ask me to come over to visit. There was something about her loss and her ability to carry on under the weight of it that compelled me to come back. I wanted to watch how she kept going. I was also intrigued by her solitary life, by how she kept herself busy. That's what I liked about her. She seemed fine not having a lot of people around. She never asked me what I wanted to be when I grew up, like other adults always did. She didn't need to chatter.

On her kitchen wall hung a cat-shaped clock with enormous blinking eyes that scanned the room like searchlights. It was the creepiest thing I had ever seen. Her kitchen served as a gardening laboratory where potato chunks and avocado seeds took root in jars of water before she transplanted them to her garden, a six-by-twelve-foot planting bed that she tended as attentively as you would a newborn. She had country ways that I found endearing and wanted to learn. Everything she used in her garden was from the earth; there were no chemical fertilizers or magic pellets. Aunt Ri would scatter dry fish bones and eggshells and coffee grounds into her garden, which gave back to her an abundant crop of vegetables.

Together we would take old shirts, faded tablecloths, dresses with broken zippers, and worn pants and cut them into squares to make a quilt. Every girl "back home" knows how to quilt, she told me.

"You take everything you can spare, all your tore-up pants, your aprons, your old work shirts, and make yourself a quilt. That way nothing goes to waste."

She was the first person I would call a recycler. I understood why my mother liked her. Aunt Ri was independent and lived a sensuous life, full of enticing smells and textures and tastes.

I never knew if she was a widow or a spinster, but she had her appetites. What she craved every Sunday evening as she ate her home-cooked meals was an hour with Tom Jones, whose variety show we watched regularly. Aunt Ri was obsessed with him, believed he was "colored," and would accept no argument to the contrary. His thick, curly hair was enough to give him away. He must be passing, she was convinced, because no white man can dance like that. The fact that he was from Wales didn't convince her. Mr. Jones being referred to as a "blue-eyed soul brother" did nothing to persuade her. During nearly every episode, she'd asked me if I thought that this would be the week his skintight pants would split. I'd say "maybe," not wanting to disappoint the old girl, but dreading the heart attack she'd surely have if that ever came to pass.

Things felt different between me and MaDear then. When I was younger, I'd tried to prove to my mother how useful and competent I could be. I took pride in being her baby, and I wanted to be the best one she ever had. Now, at thirteen, I felt not so much burdened by my responsibilities as distracted by other things, and those other things made me feel something just shy of resentment about my responsibilities. I wanted MaDear to be well, so I could be free of obligations, so my mind could wander and I could hang out at friends' houses after school. But I knew that MaDear wasn't ever going to be well. Not in the way that I wanted her to be. I knew nothing about the vagaries of the neurological system and how, through some cruel twist of genetic chance, she, of all people, came down with grand mal epilepsy. When classmates would see us together on the streets and ask, "Is that your mother?" I'd freeze a bit before answering. I never denied her, but before my soft-spoken "yes," a whole catalog of scenarios of school taunts would run through my head. That was new at thirteen.

The woman who had been everything to me just a few years ago suddenly wasn't enough—not worldly enough, not educated enough, not healthy enough, not modern enough, and in no way stylish. Her lack of strength, of influence, signified ominous possibilities for me. Who would be my advocate, my hero? Who would teach me how to be a woman in this world that was changing so rapidly? My view of the world was broadening with each year, and I wanted to kick the doors open and be a part of it. I wanted a life that was daring, engaging, independent, and productive. My idea of myself as separate from my mother and the rest of the family was something I wanted, but I couldn't imagine it with any detail. Where did I belong in the world? Where had she belonged? What does freedom feel like?

One thing we still did together was walk. Both of us were always eager to get out of the house and see what was going on in the world. Some days we'd walk down East 14th Street, past Emby's supermarket and St. Louis Bertrand Catholic Church, past Clem Daniels's liquor store to the Oakland–San Leandro border at 107th Avenue. In those days East Oakland was experiencing the last gasps of white flight, and our neighbors to the south wanted no part of the Black folks who had pushed their way deeper into the city. Having been displaced in San Francisco and West Oakland by redevelopment schemes, and by highway construction projects in North Oakland, Black folks found that there were few affordable and welcoming places left to go in the immediate area. Neighboring San Leandro was openly, shamelessly segregated. News reports of cross burnings and vandalism of Black-owned properties were an unfortunate fact of life. The city had a uniformed police officer parked on the east side of East 14th Street, and his duty, we'd been told, was to turn back any Black person coming from Oakland. MaDear and I would head south toward the old Durant auto plant several yards from the city border, where the patrolman was parked, and we'd stand there watching the cop watch us as we inched closer to the green-and-white "Welcome to San Leandro" sign. Now, we knew we had no business in San Leandro. But we also knew that whether we had business there or not was beside the point. The cop was defending his turf. We were yet to establish ours.

twelve

SPIRAL

I was in Mrs. Davis's eighth-grade math class, giggling at her psychedelic underwear that showed through her sheer white bell-bottoms. I was trying to get Maverick, Marc, and Foster to laugh. Being funny was my only social currency at Elmhurst. It kept bullies at bay and made me friends. And it gave me pleasure to make people smile. But these three were a hard audience.

Over the PA system, a disembodied voice said, "Could Dorothy Lazard please come to Mrs. Williams's office?" Mrs. Williams was the girls' vice principal.

Mrs. Davis stopped her pre-algebra lesson and nodded toward the door. I rose from my seat and headed out of the room and down the hall to Mrs. Williams's office. The old battle-ax and I had had our run-ins. More than a few times, I had wound up on the wrong side of her wooden paddle, but I couldn't guess what I had done this time. In seventh grade I was notoriously late and, therefore, sometimes locked out of class and found "loitering" in the hallway, which would get me in trouble. Or I'd answer back after a teacher felt she should have the last word, and then it would be back to Mrs. Williams and, sometimes, a suspension would follow. MaDear never seemed to mind my suspensions. I was good company.

In the month I'd been in eighth grade, I had largely reformed myself. I was on time, mostly attentive and eager to learn. I was on the honor roll. So what gives? Instead of finding Mrs. Williams in her office ready to lay into me about . . . something, I found her sitting behind her desk, very formal, very official. Her paddle was not in sight. I pushed the door farther open to enter the room and was surprised to find my Uncle Shirley seated across from the desk. He stood up when he saw me. Maybe he had come to drop off some house keys, I thought. Had I forgotten my keys? Or maybe he was there to deliver a message from Sarah or Aunt Katie.

"Hey, Ann," he said, meekly. "Well . . . I come to tell you that Sis passed away this morning."

What?

I had heard what he said—I mean, my ears did their work mechanically—but there was no comprehension. I didn't know if I was even still standing.

"D'you wanna come home?" Uncle Shirley asked.

What?

I finally found words. "When?" I had asked the same question of my oldest sister, Mary, a couple years earlier when she'd called with bad news about our father. "When did she . . . ?"

My uncle looked confused and then checked his watch. "About an hour ago," he said.

The wall clock in Mrs. Williams's office read a little after eleven o'clock. October 17, 1972.

I shook my head. No, I didn't want to go home. As much as I wanted to leave that office, I absolutely did not want to go home.

"Well," Mrs. Williams said, looking at Uncle Shirley, then back to me. "There's nothing you can do now, so you might as well go on back to class."

I glared at her. Nothing she could have said to me at that moment could have been crueler or more dismissive. Those words hurt more than any paddling she had ever given me. I wanted to say, "Fuck you, lady!" but I didn't see how that would help the situation.

I don't remember much about the rest of that day. I was stunned into silence. Nothing was funny anymore or interesting. Not even Mrs. Davis's psychedelic underwear. Nothing penetrated my brain—not French verbs or the latest recipe in homemaking class or keeping my hands on my home row keys in typing class. The only thing that was clear was the fact that I would have to go home and my mother would not be there. And she would never be there again.

MaDear had been in the hospital for about a week. For what, specifically, I don't think I knew. She was set to come home on Tuesday. October 17 was that Tuesday.

At 3:15, when the bell rang, I left the school grounds, but I didn't go straight home. I wandered the neighborhood between the house on Birch Street, where my grandmother had died, and our apartment in the cul-de-sac. I wanted to believe that if I didn't go home, what Uncle Shirley told me wouldn't be true. If I didn't go home, I wouldn't see that my mother wasn't coming home. Ever.

That day cleaved my childhood in two: the half where my mother existed in the world and the other half, which began that morning. I contemplated not going home at all, but where would I go? What happens to a child without a mother? How would I ever get back to St. Louis? Despite California's many charms, I still longed for my hometown because that's where my mother was *my mother*, not an invalid sister or child. How does one move forward without one's mother? I wanted to walk until I sorted out all of the questions that ricocheted through my brain. I was too stunned to even cry. I felt an enormous weight pressing down on my chest. I struggled to get enough air. What could I say or do to escape this feeling of drowning, of not knowing what to feel? I was an orphan. A real one now.

"Orphan," I said the word out loud to no one, trying the word on to see if it fit. "Damn!"

I thought of St. Vincent's Day Home and all the children there who were not orphaned but had been separated from their families for one reason or another. Would I now end up back there? Legitimately there? Probably not. I was too embedded in my mother's family now. Then I wondered: Are the Baskins still my family at all now that my link to them has died? In California my concept of family had taken on a whole new meaning, giving me a new identity, but, principally, I was my mother's daughter. Now I wondered who I was without her.

So many questions I couldn't answer and whose torrent I couldn't slow or dam up.

I got home close to five o'clock. Sarah was there to greet me, tearful and looking exhausted. Albert was off somewhere no one knew. Sarah wanted to know if I was okay. Her fretting made me anxious. I turned on the TV, always a source of solace and distraction, but I couldn't process anything anyone said. Thoughts crowded at a narrow portal, each waiting to be articulated, but nothing could break through.

I felt guilty about not being more responsible. If I had only walked her the last block to the day home, she would have gotten there safely. She wouldn't have broken her leg. She wouldn't have been in the hospital. She wouldn't have died. It would take years for me to free myself of this guilt, and even more years to inquire why she was in the hospital that final time. (She was in the hospital with pneumonia and, on her final night, endured a barrage of seizures. Her official cause of death was "massive pulmonary failure.")

Sarah busied herself calling our older siblings and other relatives back in Chicago, whom I hadn't seen in years. I didn't say anything to Sarah, but I was mad at her and brewing with resentment. The week before MaDear had died, I had asked Sarah if I could visit MaDear in the hospital, but Sarah, a stickler for rules, told me that visitors had to be at least fourteen years old. I couldn't understand how she thought anyone could tell the difference between a thirteen-year-old and a fourteen-year-old, but she wouldn't lie, so I was barred from seeing our mother.

No one told me what had happened at the time, but I assumed epilepsy had finally gotten the best of her. It had always been a stealthy tormentor that could strike her down without warning. One of the last times I witnessed her having a seizure, I was with her and Sarah in the kitchen of Aunt Katie's board and care home. We were chatting casually after a light lunch and MaDear got up to pour herself another cup of coffee. Turning from the stove, with saucer and cup in hand, she collapsed as heavily as if she had fallen out of the sky. On the way down, she clipped the corner of a low metal cabinet, slicing her head open at the hairline. Blood flowed freely, pooling around her head and shoulders like a halo. Sarah and I bounded into action, turning her on her side as she convulsed on the linoleum floor. We shifted her away from the cabinet and grabbed tea towels to stanch the bleeding. I never got used to the sight of blood. Its dark color was nothing like the cartoonish red I had seen in a thousand TV shows and movies. This blood was much more sinister, more foreboding, especially as it was flowing from my mother. I had wondered how many more falls she could take. It had been so long since I had seen her have a seizure, I stood frozen until Sarah told me to get a towel, any towel, to stop the bleeding. As always, MaDear returned to consciousness calm but disoriented, there but somehow not there.

Spiral

MaDear's funeral was held at St. Louis Bertrand Catholic Church, a few blocks away from our house. My mother's children from her first marriage, Samella and Simmie, whom I hadn't seen since I was about five or six years old, came from Chicago to attend the service. They commented on how much I looked like our mother, which did not provide the salve they intended. We children sat in the front row of the church. As the only practicing Catholic in the family, and the one who had made all the funeral arrangements, Sarah had the service held with a full Mass. For lapsed Catholics, the ritual of Mass may leave the heart and mind, but, somehow, it stays in the body, and it triggered the latent muscle memories in my brothers and me, who had given up on the church. We knew when to stand, kneel, sit, and cross ourselves. The priest wouldn't allow us to play MaDear's favorite song, Otis Redding's "(Sittin' on) The Dock of the Bay," during the service because it was secular music, and this decision ticked Albert and me off. But there was no budging the priest, and I suspected Sarah didn't press the issue. Samella chose to have MaDear laid out in an orange polyester dress to match the one she herself wore—a creepy decision, I thought, and not one that MaDear would have approved of. I would have put her in her favorite yellow eyelet dress with the tight bodice and flared skirt. It was sunny and made her feel "dolled up" whenever she wore it. She was so pretty in it, too. But I didn't get a vote. Albert and Simmie, who were our mother's favorite children, were inconsolable. No one was going to love them as unconditionally as she had. Their tears made my own flow more freely.

I glanced behind me a few times to see who in the family had come and how they were expressing their grief. I had a sense that the Baptist contingent of my family was being exercised in ways they hadn't anticipated—our Catholicism being another thing that set my mother and her children apart.

After the service, as I sat in the back of the funeral car waiting for my siblings to come along, Aunt Ri and her friends approached me. These old ladies, who shared seeds, plant cuttings, and wisdom with me whenever I was at Aunt Ri's place, laid hands on me now and said comforting words. They told me the Lord would provide. And I really wanted to believe them. Aunt Ri asked if I'd like to come and live with her. I thought about it for a moment, surprised that she would ask. The generous gesture broke my heart a little. But I said, "No, thank you." Despite all of her kindness toward me, I knew in my gut that Aunt Ri would not be able to handle a moody thirteen-year-old. There'd be too many rules. And I didn't want to ruin what we had going: calm, easy visits. I thought it best if I stayed with Sarah, who was younger, more tolerant, and more interested in the world beyond the house. Though I appreciated Aunt Ri's gesture, I couldn't help feeling like a charity case. I was an orphan—a new role that I had no script for.

I couldn't stand the idea of that Monday ending, couldn't stand the idea of living a day without seeing my mother's body. It was hard to believe that the body that had brought me into the world was no longer occupying space in it. But there was nothing I could do to hold back the day. It would come and go, no matter what I did. Time is merciless in that way. Just as her whole life had come and gone, my life would come and go. And I didn't realize until that day that this fact was an unassailable truth. I felt powerless knowing that there was nothing I could have done to keep her here longer.

The post-funeral repast in the African American community is an inviolable tradition. Families gather to console, reminisce, and ease their grief with food and drink and stories. At least that is how it usually goes. On this occasion, our aunts and uncles offered us no chicken or macaroni and cheese, no pound cake or punch. No pot of greens. We didn't get so much as a houseplant from our relatives. Was MaDear so insignificant in the eyes of her family, I had to wonder, that her death didn't warrant upholding this tradition? At some point Samella suggested we go down the street to Kentucky Fried Chicken and get a bucket and some sides—just enough for MaDear's children. Soon our small apartment was emptied of relatives.

My sweet MaDear was buried the next day at Holy Sepulchre, a Catholic cemetery in Hayward, a town she had nothing to do with, but where she would "spend eternity." That seemed the ultimate disenfranchisement of my mother. Burying her anywhere else would not have made having to bury her at all any easier for us, but it still stung. She could not even be laid out where she wanted to. Sarah paid for the burial with her school grant, another impediment to her education.

Returning to school a few days later, I bristled with self-consciousness. It didn't take long before a girl came up to me and asked, "Did your mother die?"

I didn't hear compassion or sympathy, only morbid curiosity, but I couldn't deny it. My mother had died. And she would be dead forever. I wondered how many times I'd have to answer this question. It was a dread that superseded all of the other dreads junior high school offers a girl. This was a blow even though I had always felt a little different from the other kids at school. I had serious responsibilities, a multigenerational set of siblings, an ancient and then dead father I didn't talk about, and a stricken mother. All of this set me apart. I was never close enough to other kids to discover that all families had problems, challenges, that all families suffer trauma and loss. I was not daring enough to insinuate myself into another kid's world. Nevertheless, I always hoped that I could become like the other kids—have friends over after school, or go on vacations to national parks. That illusion evaporated when MaDear died. I didn't know *any* kid who didn't have a mother.

It would take a while, but I would figure out how to carry on in my own singular way because I was still here. I hadn't run into traffic on East 14th Street to let some speeding car mow me down—a plan that ran through my mind the day MaDear died. *I was still here.* Still breathing painfully in and gratefully out. Still looking at my face in the mirror and seeing my mother's face. Don't destroy that last physical bit of her, I told myself. I was still in the world that had so fascinated me. There were still things to discover and love. Still people to love. Sarah was still here, hoping we'd someday make our mother proud. That had to be reason enough to hang on.

But grief, I would learn, has its own universe of emotions. Grief doesn't shrink. Life just grows bigger around it until we can tolerate it.

thirteen

WESTWARD

O ne evening a couple of weeks after MaDear's death, Sarah and I decided to go to the movies to cheer ourselves up. In fall 1972 there was only one movie we were eager to see: *Lady Sings the Blues*, starring Diana Ross in her feature-film debut. Neither of us could believe that she had been cast as a much lighter and thicker Billie Holiday, but we knew any project that Diana Ross was connected to would be quality, so we went. She was the reigning queen of Motown, after all. And we needed a break from our grief. Even the Oakland A's winning their first of three consecutive World Series championships that month made me sad because MaDear had missed some class-A baseball that I know she would have loved.

Diana Ross was pretty damn good for her first time out. And who would've guessed that Richard Pryor was such a strong dramatic actor? We swooned over Billy Dee Williams, so suave, so beautiful. It was rare to have Black people represented in such a glamorous (yet tragic) light. When Billy Dee said to Diana, "You want my arm to fall off?" the women in the theater shrieked. Sarah repeated the line all the way back home.

When we got home, joyous and satisfied, we found that our TV and stereo were gone. We had been robbed. Our cousins who lived in the apartment next door said they had heard nothing unusual. Albert wasn't at home, but that wasn't out of the ordinary.

Shortly after that, Albert left us to move to Chicago. He left no forwarding address but a huge long-distance phone bill in his wake. Sarah felt defeated. But she persevered. She found a job at St. Vincent's Day Home on 8th Street in West Oakland, working as a kindergarten teacher. After a little while she found us a place to live nearby. Our little village in the cul-de-sac had begun to sour. Too much crime, drugs, and craziness. And though it wasn't as bad as it would get, it was too much for us, a thirteen- and twenty-three-year-old, on our own for the first time. Our new place was in Oak Village, a brand-new, three-story, two-building apartment complex that occupied the entire block bounded by Brush and Market Streets and 13th and 14th Streets in West Oakland. When we moved in, the building was barely occupied. After starting out in a one-bedroom apartment, we soon moved into a two-bedroom, which we would call home for several years. Finally, I had a room of my own, a bed of my own. Stability.

Though I was intoxicated by all the newness, I couldn't bear the thought of transferring schools again. Having gone to so many schools already, I didn't want to meet yet another crop of kids. Sarah learned about a new school for the arts called Renaissance

High that was across from Laney College's athletic field, and I spent a day there to check it out. Like the High School of Performing Arts in New York City, the kids at Renaissance, all white, were being expressive in the hallways as if they were auditioning for some part in a play. The curriculum was loose and vague. To Sarah's surprise, I turned it down. I didn't see myself thriving there; it was *too* unstructured. I had also gotten used to being around Black kids, being able to blend in and disappear. I wouldn't have been able to do that at Renaissance. And I didn't want to attend McClymonds High or Lowell Junior High either. I wanted to finish out my last year at Elmhurst and graduate with the kids I had known for the past few years. I wanted to see something all the way through. It was a big deal for me to complete something. So, I promised Sarah that I'd rise as early as I needed in order to get across the entire city to Elmhurst on time. It took some doing, but I pulled myself together and out of the house, racing up 14th Street to Broadway to catch the #83 bus out to East Oakland.

This daily journey introduced me to new parts of town— Clinton Park, where Native Americans were being "urbanized"; the Fruitvale district, full of colorful shops; the corridor of light industry in Melrose; and the lovely houses of Havenscourt. I loved the long bus ride. I'd do my homework on the bus or talk to the drivers, who, once they got to know you, would let you slide if you were short a few pennies for the fifteen-cent fare. I made a point of sitting near the driver out of respect for all those people like Rosa Parks who had fought for us Black folks to sit anywhere we wanted. Not everybody was ready for this change. More than a few times, white people—women mostly—would stand in the aisle, frustrated, looking for a seat that wasn't occupied by a Black person. They didn't want to sit next to us. And they wouldn't go to the back of the bus. How the tables had turned!

Traveling through town on "Aunt Clara," as we called the AC Transit buses back then, made me feel downright worldly. I picked up conversations that I'd incorporate into stories or report back to Sarah if it was something I thought she'd like to know. Sarah was an avid newspaper reader, an *Oakland Tribune* subscriber, and a real TV news junkie. Having a newspaper around the apartment, I started to read the paper, too, and not just the *Tribune* but the *San Francisco Chronicle*, the *San Francisco Examiner*, and the *Black Panther* newspaper. Whenever anyone left any section of newspaper on the bus, I'd pick it up and read it indiscriminately—sports, opinion columns, the front page. Watching adults, I learned to fold the newspaper sections in such a way that it didn't infringe on another passenger's space.

West Oakland didn't hold the charm for me of East Oakland's densely residential districts, mainly because it didn't feel like a neighborhood. I was used to living in houses, having land around me, a grassy backyard, a front porch to sit on, or at least a stoop. Where Sarah and I landed, on the border of downtown, felt very much like a construction zone, a work in progress. We seemed to live in a netherworld there in the Oak Village apartments, neither downtown nor fully in the West Oakland that our Aunt Ruby lived in on West Street, or in the age-worn section on Campbell where Uncle Shirley once lived. Our new neighborhood was being "redeveloped" when we arrived. On the opposite side of our apartment complex, an army of construction workers moved and demolished old Victorian homes to clear space for a new freeway that would connect the Nimitz Freeway (then called Highway 17, now Highway 880) to the MacArthur Freeway (part of Highway 580). The miles-long scar in the landscape stretched as far north as the eye could see. Churches were moved from one side of the construction site to the other to avoid demolition. I watched as houses on the 700 block of 14th Street and its adjacent streets disappeared, and as our street, 13th Street, was closed off and turned into an inconsequential spur. Some of the doomed old houses bore enticing signs that read "For sale $1.00," plus the cost to move the house to land the buyer owned. Some afternoons I watched as these houses were lifted carefully onto trucks and slowly carted away to parts unknown. A different kind of migration. Sarah and I joked that we could afford the house, but that was about it.

Like us, our neighborhood was in transition. There were a lot of promises being made to the people of West Oakland then. Everything was "coming." Supermarkets were coming. Jobs were coming. Newer, affordable, modern housing was coming. Oak Center, as our section of West Oakland was called, was pocked with large vacant lots waiting to be filled in the name of "progress" and "urban renewal." Across from our apartment a large billboard on the northeast corner of 14th and Market boasted new houses coming, but several years would pass before any houses appeared on the lot. There were no modern supermarkets nearby. We often bought milk, sugar, cans of soup, boxes of grits and oatmeal from liquor stores. Sometimes we shopped at Housewives Market on 9th Street or Swan's Market on 10th Street. Both markets had been serving West Oaklanders for generations, but by the 1970s, neither offered the products or the appeal of mainstream stores like Safeway or Lucky. Housewives was seriously old-school, a prime source of meats that your Southern-born grandmother might buy, like hog maws, ox tails, or a bucket of chitlins. At Swan's, independent vendors sold a variety of items from stalls. You could buy an Easter dress, a shoe shine, a bag of candies, black-eyed peas, or a log of hog's head cheese there. It always seemed crowded, but it would serve in a pinch. When we moved to the neighborhood, I noticed right away that there were no nearby drug stores where you could buy toiletries or over-the-counter medicines, or linger, reading magazines. I missed my weekly dose of *Jet*. The block-clearing would continue and the hopeful billboards would fade and the targeted lots would remain empty into the next decade.

A few blocks away, downtown was also undergoing a transition. The downtown of a generation ago, from 8th to 14th Streets, was being gutted to make way for a new, multi-block City Center, complete with high-rise office buildings, banks, and retail stores. This major construction project lured me farther downtown, where old department stores and mom-and-pop shops on Washington, Clay, 11th, 12th, and 13th Streets, popular twenty or thirty years before, once stood. Large sheets of plywood bordered the cavernous development site, and circular holes were carved into these barriers so people could see the progress. But the progress was glacial. Weeks and months would go by and nothing noticeable would be erected. No rebar, no poured foundations. And still more and more buildings came down in the name of "progress." An old world, signs assured us, was giving way to a new one.

Buildings were disappearing just as I was discovering them. Along 14th Street, vault lights—glass bricks embedded in the sidewalks that illuminated old department store basements—were being covered up. Grand architectural beauties like the Athens Athletic Club on Clay Street were being repurposed. Downtown Oakland of the early 1970s offered a simultaneous wave of discovery and loss. Fortunately, there were stalwarts, like the YWCA and Nile Hall, that would survive this period.

Living just blocks away from downtown Oakland, I found enough distractions to occupy me. Downtown's major commercial concerns had shifted north of 14th Street, and I window-shopped along Broadway and roamed the aisles in the Liberty House and Emporium-Capwells department stores. I learned to put on layaway clothes at Hartfield's and shoes at Leeds. Holmes Books, on 14th between Harrison and Alice, offered a musty retreat where I'd spend hours grazing through old *National Geographic*s and first-edition hardback novels that had long ago lost their dust jackets. The mezzanine was stockpiled with books on the shelves, horizontally and vertically wedged into every available space. Books lay on the floor in stacks and acted as bulwarks in front of the stuffed bookcases. At the front of the store, Holmes had large glass display windows where books on certain themes were featured. It was like a museum of literature! Like the pharmacist who had let me hang out reading magazines at his place on East 14th Street and 96th Avenue, Mr. Holmes and his staff never bothered me, an avid but poor browser.

For all the age and dust of Holmes Books, the brightly lit, airy DeLauer's newsstand on Broadway offered newspapers from around the country and high-gloss, hot-off-the-press magazines about everything. There were paperback novels and crossword puzzle books, magazines on coin collecting and home decorating and guns. Interactions with customers at this venerable newsstand were quick and friendly, with one exception—me. I'd linger reading celebrity magazines like *People*, *Reader's Digest*, and *TV Guide* to see what I should look forward to that week. I read the inside and back cover descriptions of novels, but rarely did I buy anything.

I discovered the Oakland Public Library's main branch at 14th and Oak. There I loitered in the glossy world of old, bound magazines—*Ebony*, *Collier's*, *Look*, *McCall's*, and the *Saturday Evening Post*—reading about World War II military invasions, movie stars, fashion trends, New Deal programs, and the civil rights movement. There I discovered the inspired photographic work of Gordon Parks in *Life* magazine. From the Young Adult section I checked out cautionary tales like *Go Ask Alice*. I prowled the fiction stacks, picking up random books whose titles or cover designs intrigued me. In the lobby, I thumbed through scores of catalog-card drawers, trying to figure out this inscrutable system of numbers and letters. Down in the basement auditorium I attended talks about foreign travel and wildlife. The accompanying slideshows whetted my appetite for adventures.

Most importantly, I discovered James Baldwin at the main library. I read his *The Fire Next Time*, which made me feel as though the top of my head had been blown off. I had never read such calmly articulated rage and honesty and love. Baldwin made me feel as though someone finally understood both the deep love and staggering disappointment that I had begun to feel about being a Black American growing up in the later half of the twentieth century. The world was not made for us, but we were expected to adhere to its rules, swallow its abuses, and pledge our allegiance to it. Baldwin shined a light on the ambivalence, the corrosive frustration that marginalized people everywhere must feel. And his prose was beautiful! He was conversing with us. That's what made his writing so tantalizing. I could imagine him sitting across from me, legs crossed, dragging on a cigarette, as he patiently explained the state of the world to me. As I read his works, I could see him pondering the world and its endless contradictions. He inspired me to become an essayist. Essay, I discovered, was an old form of writing, derived from an even older word, from the French verb *essayer*, meaning "to try." He was trying to convey an important message to me, to us younger folks, a message we desperately needed to take in. Baldwin inspired me to wonder what I might try.

It was nearly impossible in the early 1970s not to be influenced by politics and those people who helped make sense of the chaos. The previous years had been tumultuous—the escalating antiwar protests, the chaotic end of the Vietnam War, the shame of Watergate, the rise and quick suppression of the Black Panther Party. It was hard to imagine how things could get any crazier. But all the social and political disturbance certainly led me to expect crazier days ahead. Through reading I began to see how the sheen was being buffed off of the American myth of fairness, equality, and unity. As I discovered more people who told stories of who we really are—not some sanitized, patriotic story of what we claimed to be—I grew hopeful that America would one day live up to its promises.

Cities have always intrigued me. I love how muscular they are in their energy and how beautiful they are in their variety. I love all the mysteries they hold, and the power, too. I love the rabble of cities, the mashup of people and cultures, the eternal effort to work collaboratively so everyone's needs can be met. Downtown Oakland in the 1970s was for me both fuel and fence. Wandering past the jewelry shops, the furniture stores and banks, and the watch repair shops and stationers inspired all types of daydreams of what I could someday, possibly, become—not just professionally but socially—and yet it also revealed a barrier. Beyond the glass doors, I saw only white people. White people of means heading inside Breuners department store and Irene Sargent's ladies' shop. White people picking up airline tickets from the travel agencies. During these excursions through downtown it occurred to me that I had never gotten to know my native St. Louis as well as I would know Oakland. I told myself that one day I'd return, retrace my steps down to the old Union Station, to St. Nicholas School, or to my beloved Criterion Theater, which Albert and I had spent so much time in.

I wanted to see the Gateway Arch, which was still under construction during our last days on Franklin Avenue.

Life pushes and pulls at you. Memory competes with today's business. That's what I learned from reading. It makes you nostalgic at the same time it prompts you to wonder what's next, what's around the corner. Wandering aimlessly through cities, getting to know their contours and layout, their neglected corners and privileged enclaves, their infrastructure and open lands, teaches us more than just the physical nature of a place. It shows us its political and economic character, its moral stance, and its welcome or restriction of "others."

Aside from all the construction, there was lots of political and economic turmoil to walk past. That first year in West Oakland, to get to my bus in the morning I had to navigate around a long line of agitated motorists waiting for gas that was either going up in price or running out. Twelve Arab countries had imposed an embargo on the importation of oil to the United States to protest America's support of Israel, and the result was massive gas shortages across the country. That national disturbance merged physically in my new neighborhood with a more local crisis: the newspaper heiress and Cal undergrad Patricia Hearst had been kidnapped from her Berkeley apartment by the radical Symbionese Liberation Army, the crew who had assassinated Oakland Unified School District superintendent Marcus Foster in November 1973. One of the group's demands was that Patty's wealthy daddy, Randolph Hearst, pay for food to be distributed to Oakland's poor. Within weeks, big-rig trucks were rolling into West and East Oakland to deliver bags of groceries and frozen turkeys to people who themselves had little knowledge of the Hearst family or of this radical fringe group. Near us, the food was distributed at the First Unitarian Church on 14th and Castro Streets, just on the other side of the freeway construction. Distribution points along East 14th Street in East Oakland ended in chaos as delivery men tossed out bags of food to impatient and needy crowds. At least one full-fledged riot broke out in front of Food King, which, along with other stores, was looted. These were desperate times.

fourteen

LOST BLACK BOYS

W e hadn't been in West Oakland long before we got a call from our older sister Samella in Chicago, informing us that Albert had been arrested. She didn't know yet what he had been charged with, but she swore that once she found out she'd let us know. This news sent me into a tailspin. I was immediately terrified for him, worried. I couldn't imagine what he could've done to justify jail. He hadn't been in Chicago long—maybe a year. Despite all the trouble he'd caused, and the relief I felt with him out of the house, I couldn't help but think that maybe he should've stayed here in California. The prospect of losing him was more than I could tolerate. I didn't know much about jail except from what I saw in the movies: bullying, extortion, rape, and other tortures. It was violent. I didn't think Albert, with his thin frame, would be able to defend himself against that. All I could think of was him being killed or brutalized in jail. And whatever he had done, I hoped there was some way for him to be released soon. We anxiously awaited news.

Eventually we found out from Big Simmie, Sarah's father, that Albert was not in county jail, as I had imagined, but prison—for trying to steal a cow! Cattle rustling in Chicago? In 1974?! Had he lost his mind?! Who does that? What could have been the motivation? Was he . . . in league with a butcher? Albert was in Joliet State Prison, not far from Big Simmie, who promised to visit him and let us know more information about his case and any prospects of him getting out. At the time I didn't know anyone who had gone to prison. The fact that my own brother was the first filled me with shame. This was not information to share with friends or teachers or anyone outside of the family.

Two dominant family stories mark my childhood, both stories involving boys and danger, and both so old and embedded in memory that they operate like DNA. The first story was about Paul, my phantom brother. Paul was my mother's cherished youngest son, born in August 1956. The family story goes that he was so cute, so loved, that he was always in someone's arms. People doubted he'd ever learn to walk, with so much affection lavished on him. To me, Paul was a mythic figure.

I was maybe four years old when I discovered an amber medicine bottle full of hair in my mother's dresser drawer. I asked MaDear what it was. In our house, any hair that came out of your head and into a comb or brush was immediately burned on the stove; it was bad luck to have hair lying around, we were told. So, I couldn't figure out why this chunk of hair had been saved. Gently, MaDear took the bottle out of my hand and told me that I was not to disturb it. She placed it back into the drawer just as carefully as she had taken it from me, and then she explained that it belonged to my brother Paul, who had died when he was a baby. The only tangible evidence that Paul ever existed was the curls in this medicine bottle. For a long time afterward I thought of the baby's hair in the bottle. I would learn the details some years later.

One day our grandmother convinced MaDear to let her take the cherished Paul to Chicago so our relatives there could see him, such a pretty baby. MaDear consented. They boarded the train for the six-hour ride to Chicago. I have no idea how long Paul was in Chicago or how he fared there among my mother's relations. The family story—that only my mother's older children tell—goes that Paul was toddling around one night as my grandmother played cards and drank beers with friends. He got into something under the kitchen cabinet and drank it. Mam'Ella decided it was too late to take the baby to the hospital and said she'd take him in the morning. By morning Paul was dead. As he had gone, Paul returned to St. Louis by train, but this time in a casket. MaDear never told me herself how baby Paul died, just that he was dead. The news was so startling, I didn't think to ask. And I never touched the medicine bottle again. It was something sacrosanct, like the large framed portrait of my father's mother that hung in our living room, something that shouldn't be disturbed. Sarah told me years later, when I was about ten, that Paul had gotten into something poisonous. Learning this,

I began to realize why our mother was so stricken when we weren't around her, and why her relationship with Mam'Ella was so cool. MaDear didn't need to lose anyone else.

The other story, told at various times by my mother's three oldest children, was about Emmett Till. He was a relative from their father's side of the family tree. He lived with his mother in Argo, a community just outside of Chicago, and shortly after his fourteenth birthday, in the summer of 1955, he went down to Money, Mississippi, to spend time with his great-uncle Moses Wright and cousins Simeon Wright and Wheeler Parker Jr. Samella was supposed to go on the trip, too, according to the family story, but just before piling into the car to head to the train station, the kids began arguing and Samella was made to stay home. Within days of arriving in Mississippi, the pampered only child of Mamie Till was accused of coming on to a white lady in a store—a cardinal sin in the South. Four days later, the husband and brother-in-law of the white woman burst into Moses Wright's house in the middle of the night and kidnapped Emmett. They tortured and shot the boy, then tossed his battered body, weighed down with a cotton gin fan, into the Tallahatchie River, where he was found three days later.

I had seen in an old *Jet* magazine the photos of his mutilated body lying in state. I was shocked but couldn't take my eyes off of his monstrously disfigured head and face. How does one make sense of such violence meted out on a child? On any human body? What message is a person trying to send when they engage in such desecration? Emmett's grieving mother was broken but steadfast in her determination that the world would know what these men had done to her son. His horrific, senseless murder would become international news and change the world's perception of America, propelling the civil rights movement to a new urgency. This crime not only altered how people thought about the South but how Black families parented their children, and, more tragically, how a generation of Black boys thought about their futures.

MaDear attended Emmett's funeral not knowing that a few years later she, too, would meet a train carrying her young son's lifeless body.

These twin tragedies came back to me when I learned that Albert was in jail. No. Not jail. Prison. I wondered if I'd ever see him again, wondered if he'd survive his incarceration and what lasting impact the experience would have on him. I had saved nothing of Albert's to remember him by. Not even a bottle of hair. As much as I hated to admit it, I had never imagined my brother becoming anything productive—not a teacher or lawyer or mechanic—but I never imagined him in jail either. Albert was talented, a gifted artist, but ungovernable and stubbornly unmotivated. He showed little to no interest in any academic field, as far as I could tell. I had never heard him talk about what he wanted to be when he grew up or what he liked about school (though I assumed it was art class, since he was so skilled at drawing). He dropped out of high school in the eleventh grade. His incarceration was another blow to our family. We were barely hanging on emotionally in those precarious days after our mother's death. The only solace I found was that MaDear was no longer here to see this come to pass. Stress always brought on her most violent seizures. This thought, whenever I let it surface, angered me, just thinking of all the physical and psychic energy she had spent defending Albert to our father. If Albert should die, MaDear would not be here to wail over his coffin, as Mamie Till had done for her son nearly twenty years earlier.

Little did I know that the fear and anxiety I was experiencing was being felt by so many families who didn't know where their sons were or exactly how they came to be in the predicaments they found themselves in. These lost Black boys—lost to violence, drugs, neglect, and prisons—were not some separate caste of people but part and product of all of us, I came to realize. Having a brother in jail compounded the self-consciousness I felt about coming from a family that already seemed drastically different from other families.

Albert wrote letters home, and I was glad to receive them, glad to know he hadn't forgotten me. In his letters, he never responded to my questions about what exactly he had done to get arrested. He never wrote about being afraid or about being attacked, which helped me put some of my fears to rest. At least for a while. It was not long after the first few letters that his correspondence became illogical and hard to follow. His artful, swirling penmanship belied his rambling stream-of-consciousness prose. It was clear he was trying to tell me something, convince me of something that he now believed in. He was evangelizing like the Jehovah's Witnesses who came to the door on Saturday mornings just as we'd be sitting down with a bowl of cereal and *Soul Train*. Through his letters I eventually learned that Albert had joined some kind of pseudo-Islamic sect in prison and had changed his name to a Muslim name, a move I had no doubt our mother would not have approved of. I found out only much later that the group was actually a branch of a Chicago street gang.

Reading was teaching me that every story has a catalyzing event or conflict that sets things in motion. After the conflict, there's a journey that must be taken—spiritually, psychologically, or physically—that leads to a transformation. I was beginning to understand that everyone has a journey of their own, that we all have individual lives to lead, ones that sometimes don't jibe with our family's expectations. For a time we travel along with our family of origin, then with other people—friends, lovers, and mentors—and sometimes alone. The people we meet—and yes, even relatives—are like threads weaving into and out of our lives. Albert and I may have come from the same cloth, but we weren't the same thread. He chose to run one way and I another.

fifteen

REPRESENTATION

Culturally, Sarah couldn't have picked a better area for us to live. I had always been a fiend for movies, so I was happy to find a few old theaters within walking distance of our apartment. During the early 1970s, movie theaters were being torn down for new commercial buildings, but there was still the Lux on Broadway and the Roxie on 17th Street, screening the latest from Hollywood. Sometimes Sarah and I would venture north to the MacArthur–Broadway Mall or to the Piedmont Theatre to catch a movie, but the downtown theaters were our favorites.

The Black Arts Movement, launched in the late 1960s, was at its zenith in the mid-1970s. For young people like me, coming of age during this time was more visually and ideologically stimulating than any other period in our lives. It was the first, best time to be a Black kid in this country. The Afrocentric art that seemed suddenly everywhere taught us to value our own natural, Black selves, our hair and our heritage. This mental rewiring was a challenge after so many years of being fed white standards, white images. This movement was a gift more powerful and long-lasting than any gun battle, civil rights demonstration, or political manifesto. It was foundational, demonstrating in so many creative ways that if we couldn't love ourselves, appreciate our own value, how in the world could we convince anyone else to value us?

My teen years were radically different from my early years. We had cast off the word "Negro" and begun to call ourselves "Black." That's Black with a capital B, thank you very much. It caused a rift in a lot of families across the country, with the older generation clinging to the "Negro" moniker and the slow and steady agenda of integration. Meanwhile, we young folks were declaring, as James Brown had a few years earlier, "I'm black and I'm proud." We began to realize that we had to name ourselves to claim our value. We had to change the minds of those who sought to undervalue us as a community, to bar us from what was rightfully ours. The arts movement that now centered the Black body and Black culture was predicated on reinvention. It stimulated my desire to write and to add to this amazing explosion of expression.

Sarah was a museumgoer, and I would tag along with her sometimes to check out what was on display. Art popped up everywhere in Oakland—in galleries, in people's houses, in recreation centers. The Rainbow Sign in South Berkeley was a mecca for aspiring and established Black artists—poets, essayists, dancers, singers—and the community was always welcome to partake of the art exhibits, the readings, the talks about the power of art.

What helped open up the barn doors was the new era of film-
making. In the early 1970s, on the heels of Gordon Parks's success
in directing *Shaft*, Hollywood got a sniff of the money to be made
from the Black community, and suddenly there were loads of Black-
themed films: gangster movies, thrillers, police procedurals, horror
flicks, romances. Not all of them were as well-made as *Shaft* or the
Motown-backed *Lady Sings the Blues*, but we flocked to them anyway, just as we had flocked to television sets to see Black performers
years before. We were just so happy to see *anybody* resembling us
on screen, we didn't much care about the plot of the film. A Black
private detective working a case, a Black vampire chewing up L.A.,
brothers karate-chopping their way through Hong Kong, a Black
family struggling for respect, an urban kid chasing seemingly impossible dreams. We were there for it. We were learning how to view
ourselves, magnified and beautiful. Despite all the C-grade scripts,
mediocre acting, and pedestrian directing, we were learning how to
critique these cinematic selves.

My film obsession was fueled by a trip to the Oakland Museum
in February 1973. In observance of Black History Month, the museum's Cultural Affairs Guild hosted a film festival to celebrate the
history of Black presence in American cinema. A few hundred people crowded into the James Moore Theater over a number of days
to see the wide-ranging series, which showed everything from early
Paul Robeson films (*The Emperor Jones*) to earnest, socially conscious midcentury films like *Bright Road*, with Dorothy Dandridge
and Harry Belafonte. After the screenings, Albert Johnson, a UC
Berkeley professor and film historian (who knew there was such a

thing!), showed clips from early films—*Rufus Jones for President*, featuring a four-year-old Sammy Davis Jr., and *St. Louis Blues*, with blues singer Bessie Smith—and he explained their historical significance to the audience.

The film screenings became a popular annual event at the museum, with Professor Johnson moderating the lively Q&A that followed. The talks mainly centered on Black portrayals in Hollywood—not just the ones we got but the ones we wanted. Hollywood for decades had been banking on our denigration, and the typical movie fare, if Blacks were included at all, often demeaned, abused, or sacrificed us in some way. Like most Black kids, I learned early in my film consumption that Black folks rarely made it to the end credits. We not only wanted representation, we wanted to see ourselves in all our humanity and complexity. We also wanted to see ourselves win, being resourceful and heroic. Young people condemned the old Stepin Fetchit and Black mammy movies from the 1930s and 1940s, but, to be honest, a lot of recent movie fare offered just new versions of those early "shuckin' and jivin'" portrayals that had unnerved us earlier. Instead of being set on Southern plantations or in Manhattan boudoirs, these new portrayals were in urban settings, usually drug-saturated ghettos. Simply seeing Black faces on the silver screen was not enough anymore. We wanted to see recognizable characters.

The audience peppered Professor Johnson with questions at every event: How much power do Black folks really have in Hollywood? How many Black screenwriters are working in Hollywood?

Why aren't films made by Black filmmakers getting distributed widely? How does film distribution work? How does film financing work?

Professor Johnson introduced us to early Black filmmaker Oscar Micheaux, who made independent movies on a shoestring budget in the 1920s and '30s that elevated our people, portraying them in all their psychological, class, and moral diversity. Micheaux hired Black actors, some of whom would make the leap to mainstream Hollywood films, like Paul Robeson, who, having grown disgusted with the limited opportunities in America, went to England to act in movies of substance.

During the 1970s, a period that would become known as the Blaxploitation era in film history, the debate about what type of film Black folks *should* appear in got complicated by bringing class concerns into the mix. Many in the community felt there were positive depictions (teachers, ministers, hardworking parents) that Black audiences *should* support, while other characterizations (drug dealers, prostitutes, junkies, criminals) should be condemned. The museum audience became especially charged after the screening of Melvin Van Peebles's controversial *Sweet Sweetback's Baadasssss Song*.

At the same time we were being introduced to these controversies, the independent film *The Mack*, starring Max Julien and Richard Pryor, hit theaters. Shot on the streets of West Oakland, it tells the story of an ex-con who becomes a successful pimp and the underworld life he inhabits. Despite all the hue and cry about "proper" representation, this film was very popular with Black audiences, and in the decades after its release it would continue to be highly influential in popular culture and fashion.

The film series at the museum had me buzzing, making me rethink all the movies I had absorbed and what they were not so subtly telling me about myself and my place in society. From my earliest days, I had ingested a steady diet of white victors and Black subordinates—slaves, maids, butlers, and feeble-minded, shuffling old men. Professor Johnson exhibited clips from films like *The Pirate* and *Ziegfeld Follies*, which featured Black actors, dancers, and singers in segments that were edited out when the movies were shown in segregated Southern theaters. We were dispensable, Hollywood always seemed to be telling us. Learning things like this, I reassessed all those films in which no Black people appeared, not even as servants. Each question led to more questions. How did Black actors justify working in an industry where they were so disregarded? How did any of them make a steady living with such limited opportunities? White audiences never had to search far for positive, or even interesting, portrayals. White actors had access to every type of role. I realized that all those times I'd heard Bette Davis blithely say in her films, "I'm free, white, and twenty-one," that there was cultural currency in that off-the-cuff remark, which I read as code for "I can do what I want." It was true. And I wondered when I'd see a Black woman on screen sail through life so confidently.

Some of the organizers of the museum's film festival would go on to create the nonprofit organization Black Filmmakers Hall of

Fame, Inc., which would sponsor, over the next twenty-six years, film screenings, annual film symposia, and screenwriting competitions. The organization also held at Oakland's newly refurbished Paramount Theatre a swanky annual awards ceremony, complete with star-studded red carpet reception, to celebrate Black actors, directors, producers, and other creatives working in the film industry. It felt good to see so many stars in little ol' Oakland receiving acclaim for not just excelling (like Sidney Poitier and Diahann Carroll) but enduring (like Beah Richards, Woody Strode, and Clarence Muse). The ceremony was named in honor of the trailblazing Oscar Micheaux.

Even though I was learning to look at film critically, I admittedly had a high tolerance for trash. I went to see just about anything that appeared at the Roxie, my favorite of the downtown theaters. Movies provided me with an escape. I'd rather sit in the dark in front of a huge, flickering screen, watching people do things that I couldn't do and go places I hadn't gone, than to go to an anxiety-producing school dance or a house party. Movies helped me forget, at least for a little while, my worries about Albert, my longing for our mother, and anything else that bothered me. For a couple of hours, in the dark, with a theater full of strangers, I could be someone else somewhere else. But it wasn't just the movies that I loved, it was being in a theater full of people who also loved movies. We talked to the screen, yelled out warnings to imperiled women, whistled at the handsome men, cried when our favorite characters died, and laughed when they did something dumb. I imagined we were longing for the same thing—some dreamscape to put ourselves in.

By the mid-1970s the movie ratings system that had been introduced years before but often ignored was now being rigidly enforced by local theater owners. No child under seventeen was allowed into an R-rated film without an adult, so to get into the movies I'd either go with Sarah—who didn't care for the Jim Brown/ Fred Williamson/Pam Grier action fare that I liked—or I'd ask any random adult going into the theater if I could tag along with them. I'd hand them my money before we reached the ticket booth and then scoot in behind them. People were generally cool about facilitating this ruse. It was only when I got a little older and was with a few of my girlfriends that some men, having gotten us into the theater, thought we were suddenly on a date. Yikes!

By 1976 some enterprising person tried to reopen the massive T & D Theatre on 11th Street between Broadway and Franklin. The place had been abandoned after some seedy years as a porn house and then closed again. It was now reopened in an attempt to bring the behemoth back to its former glory. The story was that in its heyday the T & D had been absolutely gorgeous, rivaling the opulent Paramount Theatre in luxury. Movie premieres were once held there. Its marquee had shone brightly. Now, its heavy velvet drapes bore generations of dust. Everything had a pallor of gray. It felt a bit like Dickens's neglected Miss Havisham, waiting to be rescued from a life of broken promises.

My cousin Jackie, my niece Vicky, visiting from Chicago, and I went to see *Cooley High* one afternoon. Admission was $1.00. And no one in the ticket booth gave two hoots about the ratings system. They let everyone in. We entered this dusty chamber of horrors, walking on the sticky, elaborately patterned plush carpet through the lobby, where we saw framed photos of the theater in its prime. Though the theater owner was trying to appeal to a wider audience, the creepy jerk-offs in the trench coats—the porn fans—were still on scene, so we were very selective in choosing our seats. Every once in a while someone on the other side of the theater would shout, "A rat!" and a cluster of folks, shrieking and giggling, would simply migrate to another section of the theater. Then it would happen all over again.

We were fully into the movie (who doesn't love Glynn Turman?!) when some dude dressed like the last pimp in California—all in white from the top of his wide-brimmed hat to his crepe-soled platform shoes—cruised slowly down the aisle. He stopped briefly to check us out, smirked his disapproval, then continued, surveying everyone as he passed, making sure that everyone saw him.

"Say, down in front!"

"Sit yo' ass down," people in the back of the theater bellowed.

The dude paused, then moved down the aisle a bit before dramatically fanning out the tails of his long white duster.

"Yeah, yeah. We see you. Now, sit down!"

I wondered what idiot comes to a show in the middle of the movie.

After much collar-popping and brim-smoothing, the guy finally took a seat. And as soon as he did, he disappeared! The entire row of seats flipped backward, and all we saw were those white crepe-soled shoes sticking straight up. Probably from Flagg Brothers, I guessed. The entire theater burst into hysterics. People pointed and laughed as the guy scrambled up from the floor, all his cool evaporated like ice on hot pavement. He walked quickly up the aisle toward the exit, all his swagger gone. The man had strutted in but crept out.

As Mam'Ella used to say, "Pride goeth before the fall."

sixteen
FINDING A VOICE

D uring my sophomore year at Castlemont High School in East Oakland, I spent some time hanging out with the wrong crowd, trying to be cool, not taking school seriously at all. High school seemed to demand that I work on sharpening my social skills and making friends. I gravitated to my old friends from Birch Street, juniors and seniors who would cut fifth period to head up to Bottleneck Liquors near the zoo. Randy, the tallest among us, went in to buy bottles of cheap liquor. Pear Ripple was our favorite. We'd sit on Las Vegas Avenue, a dead-end street behind Bishop O'Dowd High School, drinking our cheap wine, talking trash, flirting (I had a crush on Randy's cousin), and just wasting time.

I'd wander into fifth period geometry class tipsy and unprepared. Mrs. Birdie Williams, the chalk-dust-covered teacher, would glare at me as I entered and noisily took my seat. What's with the attitude, I wondered. Doesn't she know that I'm trying to be popular?

That some of us don't just wake up popular? That there's work to be done, and I'm already so far behind on all the social stuff? Needless to say, I wasn't gaining an appreciation for geometry.

A few months later I stood at the door of my geometry class waiting for a chance to talk with Mrs. Williams in private. Once the class emptied out, I stood nervously across from her with an application in my hand. I had the nerve, the temerity, to ask Mrs. Williams to write me a letter of recommendation to attend the Upward Bound Program, which prepared low-income and first-generation college students for higher education. It was being hosted by UC Berkeley that summer, and I wanted to join my friends who were applying. I held the application out, anticipating new adventures on a college campus, trying to forget my shoddy fifth period attendance and my aversion to geometric proofs. Mrs. Williams looked at me, her dark-brown face a blank slate, as if she had never seen me before.

"No." That tiny word bloomed easily from her.

Before I could protest, she offered an explanation.

"I will not write you a letter of recommendation. I'd rather write it for someone who'll struggle through the program than for you, who's been wasting your time *and* mine on foolishness. Coming into my class like you do . . . You are smart. You don't even need this program. So, no. You won't get a letter from me."

And that was that. I stood before her stunned, feeling deprived. She looked at me, directly. For the first time, standing near her, I looked at her. I didn't shift my gaze. I let her word wash over me, sink into my skin. No. So much power in those two letters. I was suddenly contrite. Besides not learning geometry—whose value I couldn't figure out on even my most clear-headed days—I had been disrespectful to this woman who had only tried to make me smarter. I walked away disappointed but also ashamed of myself after hearing her sobering truth. I was, she was telling me, what I had always wanted to be: smart. Mrs. Williams had seen it. And I, in an attempt to be a part of a group, had ignored it, cast my intelligence and curiosity aside, cast my ambition aside, and why? So that some boy might like me?! As one of only a few sophomores in geometry class, I should have taken that as a clue that I was smart. But I didn't know how to push myself. As long as I was getting good grades, my family thought everything was fine. They didn't push me with incentives or ideas of what possibilities lay ahead. And I had begun to steer away from any teacher who might push me, especially the women teachers, who I was afraid to get near. I didn't want pampering or anything that smacked of preferential treatment. I realized that I got really lazy whenever I was scared of something I deemed too challenging. Like geometry. I didn't know how to ask for help, feeling that to do so would be to reveal a deficiency. Certainly, at times, I needed help and should have asked for it. I was trying to figure out who I was in this new environment of high school. I was rudderless in a big sea of possibilities.

For a long time I thought about Mrs. Williams's words. They were so hurtful, but also effective. A "no" can be as much a motivator as a "yes." She got me thinking about how I presented myself. It wasn't enough to be the class clown, or even the self-effacing wallflower. I had to take myself seriously, at least more seriously than

I had up to that point. I wanted things: namely, to have a safe and bountiful life, but I also wanted freedom and movement. And, though I would never say so out loud to anyone, I wanted to be loved.

It was shoulder to the grindstone after Birdie Williams's rejection. I pulled my act together and got serious about being serious.

That first Christmas in West Oakland Sarah bought me a journal and I started a daily habit of writing. That practice took me back to my steno pad days in San Francisco. But unlike those days when I was looking at everything and recording what I saw, now I was looking inward and recording what I felt. Journaling helped me settle down better than any attempt at socializing because it gave me a means to say how I was feeling, safe from taunts, judgment, or concerned admonitions. Writing, seeing my words on paper, demanded that I be honest, that I connect the right words with my emotions. Those hardbound journals I received every Christmas from Sarah gave me a safe place to practice voice. After losing MaDear, I didn't know what to say about anything anymore. I couldn't figure out why, after so many years of being hospitalized and returning home to us, her body had given out when it did. She was only fifty. Her death had silenced me for a while, blocking my access to stories. My curiosity waned. But now, with a journal, I was finding motivation and clarity. I came to some understanding about time and how fleeting it is and how unconsciously we live despite it relentlessly ticking away.

All writers need inspiration. I discovered the Oakland Ensemble Theater, a Black company a couple of blocks from our apartment. The creative people who ran it welcomed students by offering drama classes, free tickets to plays, and opportunities to work in the theater. I encouraged my friends Angie Mitchell and Rhonda Dunwood to join me there to check it out. I had begun to write scripts, following the model of plays I read. Given the quality of most of what I was seeing on the screen, I figured I could easily write a screenplay (though I didn't know where to send one once I finished). I had learned the orthodoxy of episodic television long ago, and now my attempts at screenwriting led to other forms. I wrote monologues and short stories. I started a novel. I wanted Hollywood to do right by Black folks. Though we were on TV more than at any other previous time, there were still a lot of stereotypes, buffoonery, and one-dimensional characters. I wanted to contribute what I could to turn things around.

I was particularly drawn to those socially relevant movies produced during this time, movies about the abuse of power in government, threats to the environment, the manipulative mass media, and labor issues. Movies back then showed people working, earning a living, and facing moral challenges. Besides the news, movies let me know that there was a lot of work to do to make our society what it claimed to be: fair, open, and accountable. The best movies of the 1970s—movies like *The China Syndrome*, *All the President's Men*, and *Blue Collar*—were filled with righteous indignation about the state of the world and shined a spotlight on average citizens having agency, working to make life safer and more just, not always winning but becoming enlightened about their place in it. There were lots of important subjects out there to tackle.

Maybe it was the influence of Woodward and Bernstein's reporting on the Watergate scandal, or of Cary Grant and Rosalind Russell in *His Girl Friday*, that made me consider journalism. Sarah watched TV news religiously and talked about it with me, helping me see how world and national events had major implications locally. Everything was connected somehow to everything else, and it was also crucial to pay attention to the way those events were reported, or *not* reported. I wanted to write stories about underreported topics. I wanted to do something that would bring Black stories out of the shadows. There was lots going on during those years that I never saw a network newscaster or mainstream print journalist investigate in any detail—stories like the forced sterilizations of Black and Puerto Rican teens, or what the Black community thought about abortion, or the self-reliance in the Black community that existed long before the federal antipoverty programs. I figured it would be an ideal field for me, as I had cultivated a pretty sharp fly-on-the-wall persona. That seemed to be a perfect trait of a journalist, this ability to not make oneself the center of the story but to be an observer and recorder of events.

Thanks in part to Mrs. Birdie Williams providing me with that "come to Jesus" moment, I focused on school during my junior year at Castlemont. I was elected class historian, a position that called for me to advertise school events (many of which I didn't attend because they were often at night and Sarah and I had no car), take notes at student government meetings, and things like that. My creative writing teacher, Elaine Kachavos, inspired me to keep writing. And I did. I was journaling daily. There was lots to write about, too. In January, the great actor, singer, and activist Paul Robeson died, leaving a void in the world a mile wide, and I, having just read his book *Here I Stand*, wrote about him as my ideal of a courageous, intelligent, politically astute, humane figure. In February, I wrote about the freak snowfall in Oakland. I jotted down my thoughts about the upcoming presidential election, which pitted a Georgia peanut farmer against an incumbent president no one had voted for. But most importantly, that year's Castlemont basketball team won the Tournament of Champions, which sent the entire school into a frenzy. The Castlemont Knights beat Balboa High for the championship, and although I'd only managed to go to one of the games, it was a thrilling experience. Lots of school spirit on display.

Parties were thrown all over East Oakland, and cousin Donna convinced me to go to a few. Years after my arrival in California, I was still dependent on Donna for social connections. One night, we hitched a ride up to a party on Castlewood Avenue in the Oakland hills, not far from the Oakland Zoo. I had no idea who was hosting this party, but, like so many others looking to celebrate our championship, we crashed it. Couples were in bathrooms, bedrooms, everywhere, getting personal. Like me, Donna wasn't much for dancing, and so amid the weed haze and the drinks and the mingling, we settled in, mostly just waiting for some reliable way to get back down the hill to her house. We sat together in an egg-shaped chair equipped with surround-sound speakers and watched the proceedings, grooving to the music. It was so cozy and relaxing in the darkened living room. We woke hours later, near dawn, rousted by someone's mother asking us where we should be.

"You don't have to go home," she told us, "but you gotta get outta here!"

We scattered and walked the two miles all the way to Donna's house on 77th Avenue.

I was re-elected class historian in my senior year. (I don't think anyone else wanted the job.) I loved it because it gave me an opportunity to practice my graphic design skills (hand-drawn in those days!). I also joined the newspaper crew and was assigned to be the editor of *Ye Castle Crier*—my first stint in a power position. Working on the school newspaper made going to school fun. I loved gathering stories, the opportunity to inform a community, and the chance to learn something new every day. My tendency to float between the disparate worlds of the high school solar system all seemed justified once I was the editor. I hung out with members of the track team and the honor society students. I was friendly with the basketball jocks and members of the Castleers, our school's famous choir. Feeling I belonged in no particular place, I could drift in and out of nearly every orbit. I knew how to make friends and, when comfortable, keep them. Living outside of Castlemont's residency district was a practical inconvenience, but it also helped me steer clear of

Accepting an award for my work on Castlemont High School's
newspaper, *Ye Castle Crier.*

the cliques and gossip that led to conflicts. I developed my own routines and kept myself busy.

Like most teens, I wanted to be unique. I had carved out a persona for myself at school: the smart kid who could be funny and
disruptive, though my clowning in class had subsided—a bit. (I
still enjoyed roasting Mr. Fergus, my French teacher.) My sartorial
tastes swung wide. One day I'd be in jeans, tee shirts, and knit caps.
The next day I might be in a tailored suit. I often wore my hair
in rolls and buns, copying the Pointer Sisters' 1940s style that was

popular at the time. I was growing more comfortable in my own skin. I was no longer ashamed of being smart or unpopular with the boys, who tended to see me as a buddy, a kid sister, or a source for other girls' phone numbers. I saw boys as an impediment to the freedom I desperately desired. Getting too close to them, you could wind up pregnant or heartbroken or both, as some of my friends had. Freedom was just around the bend, and I wanted no one in my path. I embraced my love of solitude, my bookish routines, and my ambition because it made me feel good, focused, powerful. It made me feel like I had control over my life, just like Mr. Chatman had control over his gymnast body. Inside my head, I was the queen of my own nerdy domain.

Writing was paying off, helping me build my confidence. During my last semester of senior year, the television miniseries *Roots* aired. Based on Alex Haley's 1976 fictionalized telling of his family's history, this was a major television event. Over seven days, *Roots* broke all kinds of viewing records, averaging about thirty million viewers per night. It was revolutionary in its depiction of American slaves, showing the brutality and family disruption inherent in slavery. It was a unique program in that it told a Black American story *not* beginning at the plantation, as had every other program I'd ever seen set during that time. Instead, it began in an African village, focusing our attention on an intact, multigenerational African family living in a thriving African society. Before the white captors showed up, we saw African birth customs and maturation rituals, intergenerational relationships, and some of my favorite actors. Sarah and I were riveted.

Some months later, I entered a "What *Roots* Means to Me" essay contest sponsored by the San Francisco African American Historical and Cultural Society. I entered the contest as a wave of interest in genealogy crested over the country. Most Black Americans had no idea where their families originated in Africa, but the fact that Alex Haley had been able to discover the origins of his own family dispelled the general belief that it was impossible to do. People were tantalized by the prospect that their broken origin stories might not remain broken forever. Through years of research and interviews and transcribing family stories, Alex Haley had traced his family's story all the way back to the Motherland, Africa. No, not just Africa—specifically, Gambia, the village of Juffure. It was an amazing feat by any measure. He could say in no uncertain terms where he had come from—what village, what people.

What did *Roots* mean to me? I had to ponder that question with considerable energy. I had not thought about my family in terms of ancestors. According to my birth certificate, my father was sixty-eight when I was born. That fact alone kind of made him my ancestor. Was his mother or grandmother a slave? What had he learned of slavery from them? I hadn't thought about his mother and what her life must have been like. Having lost contact with my half-siblings in St. Louis years before, during all the family's moving, I knew these questions would likely remain unanswered. The phone numbers Mam'Ella had kept in her phone book had been lost long ago, and the ritual of letter writing had been put aside. No one was asking for letters anymore; the tradition seemed to have died with Mam'Ella.

Roots made me contemplate my father's life in a more serious way than I was able to even when he died. I knew so little about him, about the family he came from. I knew his mother's name was Mary and that she was a cook like him. I knew he had suffered a large burn on his forearm, which he told me he had sustained from playing around a big boiling kettle when he was a boy. But what of his father? His siblings? I knew he had sisters, but I didn't remember ever meeting them or asking their names. Were they still alive? Could they be? Our significant age difference had curbed my curiosity about his life.

These gnawing questions with their irretrievable answers fueled my *Roots* essay. In it, I advocated for people to talk more with their relatives about their family history. The whole exercise made me wish I had spent more time talking with Mam'Ella and Aunt Ri about their lives as young women in the rural South. The history that I sought out so avidly in books and magazines and on TV had chroniclers and participants in my own family, and I had squandered the opportunity to gather their stories, thinking the big and important stories belonged to other people elsewhere.

Learning African American history built my self-esteem by confirming that I had a place here in this country. That history demonstrated to me that no matter what horrific, illegal, violent, criminal shit America has thrown at us, we've managed to thrive, to create, to flourish in so many fields of endeavor. I had a right to be here and an obligation to be all I could be. *Roots* made me realize how empowering knowing one's family history is. My ancestors, known or unknown, as Baldwin so eloquently argued, paid for my place in this world. They suffered enslavement, racial terror, degradation, discrimination, ignorance, poverty . . . It was humbling to think about.

My essay was about the absence of information, the longing to know, the missed benefits of knowing. Having no story, I decided, *was* a story.

To my surprise, I was picked as one of the contest winners. The prize was a certificate and a banquet dinner with Alex Haley himself. Mr. Haley gave a speech on the importance of history and the value of knowing where you came from. After the chicken dinner and speech, we aspiring essayists each received an autographed hardbound copy of *Roots*. In my copy, Mr. Haley wrote: "To Dorothy Lazard, from the family of Kunta Kinte."

seventeen

MOTHERMOTHERMOTHER

Sometime during my senior year of high school, it dawned on me that I had forgotten the sound of my mother's voice. I was not only forgetting the things she said but the tone and timbre of her voice, the blast of her rare laughter, qualities that made her voice uniquely her own. This revelation left me feeling horrible, as though I had somehow, unwittingly, killed her for sure. Had I crammed so many voices into my head that that essential voice, that first family voice, was replaced in my brain? And by what? Stevie Wonder on an endless spool? Mike Douglas singing some decades-old standard? Pam Grier saying, "Get back, sucker!"? Whose voice had replaced my mother's voice?!

After MaDear's death there seemed to be no amount of contrition I could make to ease my guilt about not having been a more attentive, loving, accepting daughter. It created in me a reluctance to be around women my mother's age, particularly those who might, in some way, show me any maternal inclinations. I veered away from them, ignored most of their party invitations, their offers of babysitting gigs or trips to cultural events. I didn't physically dodge them; I simply declined their offers of mentorship, friendship, and advice. I didn't want to be the girl who needed special care or a handout. For a time, it felt like everyone knew I was orphaned, as if I had a big embroidered *O* on my chest. And I was embarrassed—even though there wasn't anything I could have done to prevent the deaths of my parents. The attention of older women only increased, rather than eased, my self-consciousness. Avoiding them wasn't something I planned, but my gut told me to tread lightly into this territory.

At friends' houses, I was curious about the mother-daughter relationships I witnessed. I noted the tensions, the teasing devotion, the care, the confidence they had to move through the world because they were someone's mother and someone's child. They had advocates and devotees. They seemed to have a societal currency that I just did not have. I envied my friends for their present and capable mothers. But was "envy" the right word? I didn't want just anyone's mother; I wanted my own.

Often I would strike up conversations with my friends' mothers about any old thing, just to get them talking. I would imagine what my mother would think about the latest fashion, or the news out of the White House, or the traffic. I wanted them to show interest in me at the same time that I wanted to be invisible. My friends' mothers liked me, for the most part. I was mannerly, quiet, plain enough not to be threatening, and a good student. A loyal friend.

I couldn't understand why my friends complained about their mothers, saying they were too strict, too old-fashioned, too . . . something. Didn't they know that in an instance this treasured, anchoring being could very easily be wiped off the face of the earth? And then what would they do? Wouldn't all the silly arguments about clothes and hair and the "right" boy hanging around seem a stupid waste of time?

When my friend Angie Mitchell, whose family had moved to Oakland from Omaha in the middle of eighth grade, announced that her family was moving and that she'd have to transfer from Elmhurst to Havenscourt Junior High for ninth grade, I was crestfallen. Angie and I had become fast friends, and finally I was the one who could show someone else the ropes. I was no longer the new girl at school. We had made friends shortly after my mother died, and I found comfort in her not knowing about that before we became friends. I didn't have to worry about her feeling sorry for me, or whispering about my loss and what it could mean. Our friendship was clean. So, with that in mind, I petitioned Mrs. Mitchell with all the force of a trial lawyer to let Angie continue at Elmhurst. Everyone and everything seemed to be moving all the time, and although I couldn't seem to stop this perpetual motion, I wanted to try. Mrs. Mitchell told me she appreciated my advocacy and was glad that Angie had made such a loyal friend, but no, she would not reconsider. Angie was going to Havenscourt. They were moving into Havenscourt's residency district, and that was that. Mother as sentencing judge. Even though I was heartily disappointed in the verdict, the exchange innervated me. I had never begged for anything so forcefully. I *needed* a friend who would stay put. The thought of losing this friend, of losing anything else, was more than I thought I could bear, but I did bear it. And, as Mrs. Mitchell said, I'd be fine.

Sarah was now my legal guardian. Her name was on my emergency contact list at school, on scholarship applications and job applications and a hundred permission slips and excuse-of-absence notes. It had been that way for a little while, but once MaDear was gone, really and truly gone, my sister's curvy and careful signature took on greater significance. She was, for all intents and purposes, my mother now, an indisputable fact that I both welcomed and railed against. I don't think either of us knew fully what it meant when we were suddenly alone together, just the two of us in the apartment with no elders to take on the responsibility for our care. Sarah was generous and supportive, always conscious of modeling good behavior, but I couldn't help thinking that I was a burden on her. I couldn't help wondering what she could be doing instead, who and where she'd be, and who she'd be hanging out with if she didn't have to deal with me. I was moody, sarcastic, foul-mouthed, and petulant as a teen. That eagerness that I had once felt to fit in now dissipated during my junior and senior years. I knew how to keep my own company. I had a TV and art supplies in my room, access to a phone, free run of the kitchen. I was safe. Fortunately, Sarah and I got along pretty well most of the time. We were birds of a feather, our own petite flock. We were the "eggheads" of the family and withstood a lot of mocking because of it. That was always part of the price we paid to become educated. So much of what we were learning we didn't share with many family members because they would get bored, or say we were putting on airs, or utter the most tragically illogical thing: "You think you white." So, to avoid all that, we kept to ourselves. We got by on Sarah's salary and my Social Security checks (my father's benefit), which I would keep getting till I reached adulthood. We saved coupons. We redeemed soda bottles at the liquor stores. We made each other hearty pots of spaghetti, chili, and cheesy spinach lasagnas, meals that stick to the ribs. We celebrated little achievements by going to the movies or making layer cakes or putting something on layaway at Montgomery Ward or Hartfield's.

As our extended family scattered to other parts of Northern California—San Jose, Sacramento—Sarah and I sheltered contentedly on 13th Street. Uncle Shirley kept a paternal eye on us. He'd occasionally come by to visit and give us unsolicited advice while rifling through our fridge. Sometimes he'd come with his wife, Alexzine, whom we really liked. Any visit from them usually left us laughing until we cried. They were always bickering, but their love for each other was obvious despite all their displays of irritation.

"Baskin, come out of they 'frigerator. They don't need you eating them out of house and home," she'd scold.

"Woman, these are my nieces. I wanna see if they can cook. What you got in here, Sarah? You ain't got no hot sauce in this house? Why haven't you gone to the store to get some hot sauce? What else you got to go with this chicken?"

"You don't need to see nothing up in there," Alexzine would say. "That's why you fat now. Always eating."

"Who . . . who you calling fat?! I know you ain't calling nobody fat, big as you is!"

Sarah and I never minded the verbal jousting or the invasions of our kitchen. It was like a family toll that we happily paid because we knew those two would do anything for us.

Uncle Shirley was important to us and all our cousins. He was the surrogate dad of our clan. Whether you had no dad or a deadbeat dad, he was there to help you out, sort you out, or chew you out whenever you needed it. He took care of everybody in one way or another, at one time or another. So Sarah and I didn't mind his occasional trespasses. We knew he was good for a ride or a loan or a laugh. It felt good to know that he was watching over us. He and Alexzine were proud of us, always encouraging us to go as far as we could with whatever it was we wanted to do. He hugged us like there was no tomorrow, and always boasted about having come to save Albert and me from "that orphan home."

Like our Uncle Melvin, who was the first in our family to come to California, Sarah was a pioneer, one of the first in the family to go to college. She started taking night classes at Cal State Hayward after her day shift working at St. Andrew's Community Child Care Center in West Oakland. With me able to take care of myself, and usually sequestered in my room writing or watching TV, Sarah could focus on her studies. She was finally gaining traction with her education. And like I had done years earlier, I watched her—though I pretended not to. (What's with teenagers?!) She was a diligent student, but not a great speller; and that's where I came in, like the cavalry, to save the day. I listened while she hosted study groups in our living room, and I browsed through her books when she wasn't around. Through her, I discovered John Hope Franklin's *From Slavery to Freedom* and Nikki Giovanni's poems and Maria Montessori's ideas on early childhood development.

After years of hard work, Sarah graduated with a bachelor's degree in history from Cal State Hayward. She continued her studies there and earned a master's degree in education in 1976. She was finally on her way.

eighteen
END AS BEGINNING

I was an impatient teen. I guess all teens are eager to get to that coveted next step, adulthood. I raced through school, taking summer classes whenever I could, trying to catch up to the friends who were in the class ahead of me. As a junior, I went on the school-sponsored bus tour of Southern California colleges to check out my options. San Francisco State University had a fine journalism program, but it was too close to home and, besides, I had already lived in San Francisco; I wanted something new.

At the start of my senior year I had only one required class left to take, American government, to fulfill my graduation requirements. The rest of my courses were what I'd call essential but certainly not academic—journalism, photography, printmaking, creative writing, and, as always, French. As for being a high schooler, I couldn't wait to get past the social insecurity, the boring conversations about clothes and boys and famous people we'd likely never meet.

What You Don't Know Will Make a Whole New World

Printmaking during my last year of high school, when I leaned hard into the arts.

I didn't know what adulthood would bring, but I also knew I didn't want to be dependent on anyone anymore, not emotionally or financially. I vowed privately to make it to "the other side of youth" intact. Cracked, for sure, but not broken. The only way I saw to do that was to get smart and get out of Oakland. I read distance as success. Baldwin had to go to France. Langston Hughes traveled the world. Maya Angelou went to New York. The college option sometimes felt like an escape rather than an obvious and voluntary next step in my education. I wanted *experience*, the stuff all the writing guidebooks said you had to have in order to become a good writer. Write what you know, they urged. Well, at seventeen, I only knew that I didn't know much of anything.

End as Beginning

I had always been interested in history and would try to incorporate that in any writing I did. I knew that there would always be cause to write about politics, race, and the challenges Blacks and other minorities faced in this country. I knew what risks lay in the path of any girl or woman in this handsy, misogynistic world, so I'd never run out of things to say about women's lives. I knew that the world's bookshelves were filled with stories describing lessons of loss, estrangement, and adaptability, but I had not yet realized my own connection to those experiences. I foolishly never looked at *my* life as something anyone would want to read about.

When I approached my high school counselor, Mr. Darling, to get permission to graduate a semester early, he asked if I had a job. I told him I did not, but that I could get one quickly enough. Oakland, at the time, was teeming with jobs thanks, in part, to the federal Comprehensive Employment and Training Act (CETA) program, which offered public-sector jobs to low-income students. It had supplied me with my first job the previous year as a mail clerk in the county's welfare department. I imagined getting a cashier's job at a department store or at one of the shops at Eastmont Mall. A job at a fast-food joint wouldn't be so hard to land. But his "no" was enough to block my early-graduation bid. While many of my fellow seniors were taking chemistry and calculus and prepping for the ACT (a standardized test that I avoided like the plague), I was in the darkroom developing film in Mr. Wade's photography class, or laying out the school newspaper with Ms. Washington, or learning how to make various knots in my macramé class. Anything that didn't involve the literary or visual arts held little interest for me.

What You Don't Know Will Make a Whole New World

The challenge of the trailblazer is that you don't have much information about the territory before you. In my last year of high school, I felt as I did during my first years in California: brand-new and ignorant about the way things work. I didn't know if I'd be able to adapt to this world I was lunging toward. And I was often too self-conscious to ask many questions of my elders, for fear of revealing my ignorance or of being seen as unprepared or unacceptable.

A white envelope arrived at the house addressed to me from the National Council of Teachers of English, in Illinois. Opening it, I was surprised to discover that I was one of seven Oakland students selected as winners of their student writing award, a national honor for myself and Castlemont. After that achievement, the offers from colleges came flooding in from places I had never heard of—Whitman College in Walla Walla, Washington; Agnes Scott College in Georgia; a private school in eastern Missouri. I was honored but confused about what to do, who to talk to about my choices. I wondered what the other regional winners were doing with their options, sure that they had parents who had gone to college and could guide them to the right decision. I couldn't help feeling out of my league when I read through the campus prospectuses, seeing how much colleges cost. I felt poor in a way that I hadn't in a long time.

Sarah and I had neither the money nor much information about these opportunities that she, unfortunately, never had to deal with. Some schools offered full scholarships, but they were in places I couldn't imagine myself—the Deep South, the Pacific Northwest. The offer from the University of Missouri tempted me briefly with its well-regarded journalism program, but it was many miles away from St. Louis. I didn't know anyone there. But then, when I thought about it, I didn't really know *anyone* in St. Louis anymore either, having drifted away from my much older half-siblings there.

Despite all of Sarah's care and attention, I couldn't ignore the fact that I was vulnerable and scared. An undeniable truth. I was winning awards for writing, for excelling in French, for leading the school newspaper crew, and I felt good about my achievements, but I was reluctant, always, to take the next steps, to push myself further, as far as I often wanted to go. I wouldn't join a club or an athletic team or a drama class or a choir. I let people believe— and tried to convince myself—that I was antisocial. But that wasn't really the case. Sure, I could take or leave people, but when I was with them, I usually enjoyed myself. But I was not well. All the joking, the sarcastic comments, the efforts to make people laugh were really just an attempt to claw my way out of my darkening state of mind. That blanket of sadness that I wouldn't talk about was growing tighter around me. I avoided most anything that would end in some kind of public award ceremony or performance, because each such occasion would remind me that my mother was not there to see me, that she was missing out on the happiness and pride my achievements might bring. And that would make me so miserable, especially when some friend's mother would say, "Dorothy, where is your mother? I'd love to meet her. She must be *so* proud."

She probably would be. But I'd never know. And that undeniable fact made me avoid so much joy during that time. I curbed
my ambitions because, I felt, what was the point? She wouldn't be
there to crow about my achievements, as she had done about my
good health when I was a child. She never got to see me graduate
from any school, never got to see me presented with one award.
With Sarah taking night classes, I attended most public ceremonies
and school events alone. I didn't want to fly solo anymore, but I
would accept no surrogacy; the choice bound me in solitude and
depression.

I was looking for a place to start over, to be new one more time, but
on my own terms—which had yet to be defined. That's the paradox
of youth: we want things to change and at the same time we want
to feel safe and stable. But growth, I was to learn, is rarely comfortable. I still felt that San Francisco State was too close to home, and
so when the University of Southern California offered me enough
scholarship money to get me through that first year, I jumped at
the chance to get away. The school had a journalism program, and
that was enough to convince me to take the leap. I wanted to be
near some of my old high school friends who were attending other
Southern California schools. They had introduced me to the notion of "made family," friends who were close and supportive like
family, and I wanted to be a part of that.

I would be entering territory for which I had no map. USC was for children of monied, college-educated people. Recruiters had told me during the college tour that actors John Wayne and Marlo Thomas had gone there, which did not impress me one bit. But what resonated with me was that O. J. Simpson had gone there. Sarah was in love with O. J., the star Buffalo Bills running back, and felt that if he, a Black kid from the Bay Area, could make it there, so could I. I was no rich kid or star athlete, but there I'd be, too, ready or not.

On a warm night in mid-June 1977, 550 Castlemont seniors filed alphabetically into the cavernous Oakland Auditorium arena to graduate. We sat restless in our purple and white robes through speeches and award presentations while thousands of family members and friends, high up in the stands, looked on. Sarah, Aunt Katie, Aunt Noonie, Simmie's wife Margie, Samella, and Donna came to see me reach this milestone. The only thing about the ceremony that would stick in my memory is our principal, Mr. Winston Williams, concluded his speech with, "If you want to be a ditch digger, why, be the best ditch digger you can be!" This sent giggles through the rows of

The hopeful graduate.

graduates. I could imagine all the parents squirming upon hearing this less-than-ambitious advice, but I got what he was saying. Not all of us are going to be doctors or lawyers or professors, but we should try to be the best at whatever we chose to do. I certainly planned to follow his advice.

I enrolled in summer school at Laney College a week after graduation, selecting journalism as my first college course, something I knew I'd excel in. I planned to declare journalism as my major once at USC.

Over the summer, I gathered all the things I wanted to take to college with me—my Stevie Wonder, Rufus, Pointer Sisters, and Billy Joel albums, my James Baldwin essays, my ceramic Snoopy pencil holder, my journals, my tattered copy of Paul Robeson's *Here I Stand*, the school supplies Sarah and I had bought at J. J. Newberry's, my Famolare shoes, my soft-focus inspirational posters, my beloved Zenith Sidekick TV covered in denim, the official fabric of the 1970s. It felt weird to be the one leaving instead of the one being left behind. But it was also empowering in a way that I could not fully grasp. This would be the first time I'd move to a destination I had chosen. As it turned out, leaving Oakland was easier than I had expected. With Sarah and the rest of the Baskins there, I knew I would always have a reason to come back. But I'd taken the first steps toward making my life the adventure I had always dreamed it could be.

"Uncle's baby's going off to college! Going to get her an education!"

Uncle Shirley insisted on driving me down to my new digs in Los Angeles. I had secured lodging in a large Victorian that would house seven other students, including my high school friend Patricia Coutee. Sarah and I crammed all of my stuff and ourselves into Uncle Shirley's station wagon and headed south down Highway 5. Our older sister Samella and her three children had moved to L.A. from Chicago the previous year, so I would have some family nearby, and that seemed to ease Sarah's mind; I wouldn't be without a safety net, without Sunday dinners and someone to show me around. This was also my chance to bond with Samella, my mother's first child, who was twenty years older than me. It was all settled except the part where I'd have to make and negotiate friendships, learn to budget, cook all my own meals, and select and pass my classes.

We were on the road again, Uncle Shirley and me. So much had happened in those nine years since we were last on a highway together, traveling through new landscapes toward fresh possibilities. In 1968, MaDear, Albert, and I were being rescued, or at least that's how the adults in my life saw our departure from St. Louis. This time I was being launched, full of all the lessons elders had taught me about loyalty, hard work, responsibility, and self-pride. I left Oakland full of dreams of becoming a responsible, gainfully employed journalist. Perhaps a screenwriter, too. As we made our way south through the sprawling Central Valley, waves of heat and sadness tempered the exhilaration of migration. Another milestone MaDear would miss, another place I'd live without her having been there. I thought of

MaDear, gone now for five years. Would I have made the decision to leave Oakland had she been alive? Probably not. But I *was* leaving Oakland, the place she had last lived. The last place *her* mother had lived, too. What legacy of theirs would I carry into the future?

"Girl, you look just like your mama," Uncle Shirley said out of the blue. I realized this routine observation was meant to cheer me up, to connect us. He missed his beloved older sister, maybe as much as I did. Hugging me, he tried to transmit to me all that she could not. But it was a bittersweet gesture.

I thought of Mam'Ella, too, and had to smile as I remembered something she had said to me often—and was absolutely right about: what I didn't know would make a whole new world. And here I was, hurtling toward it. I would have to learn to look at being new, at starting over, not as a loss or a deprivation but as an opportunity, an opening. Moving forward, I would have a greater degree of agency than I'd ever had before in my life. This life of mine was becoming *my* responsibility. The thought was thrilling. The reality was humbling.

We drove through the steep stretch of highway called the Grapevine, where I noticed no signs of grapes, fruit stands, or vineyards. Then we descended down into the vast Los Angeles Basin. I didn't know what awaited me in Los Angeles, at this ivy-covered private university with its celebrity alumni. It felt so far away from Franklin Avenue and St. Vincent's Day Home and the ragamuffin Haight-Ashbury and my downtown Oakland haunts. Despite the distance, I knew I'd always be tethered to Oakland, no matter how far I roamed, because I had skin in the game here. And for that reason Oakland would always be home ground.

Afterword

After my freshman year at USC, I headed back to the Bay Area, in my pursuit of a journalism degree. I enrolled at Laney College in 1978, a watershed year for local journalists (the Moscone-Milk assassinations, the Jonestown massacre), then transferred to San Francisco State University. My plan to declare journalism as my major didn't stick. Fortunately, my love of writing did. I graduated from San Francisco State with an English/creative writing bachelor's degree and, subsequently, earned a master's degree in library and information studies from UC Berkeley.

I completed this memoir a few months after retiring from the Oakland Public Library, the site where so many of my teen curiosities were fed. During my twenty years working as a reference librarian there, I hosted popular travel and history series, mounted exhibits, wrote blogs, and worked as the head librarian of the Oakland History Center. Helping people find long-lost relatives and discover family and Oakland stories helped me realize just how much of my own family history I didn't know and how much I had simply forgotten. The story you've just read is my recovery mission to retrieve a time in my life that marked me more deeply than any other. That first California decade set me on a path of discovery— of myself and the world around me.

The adventurous life I'd imagined for myself as a ten-year-old has been realized. I still love histories, films, gardening, and travel. I've snorkeled in the Indian Ocean, camped on the Baja Peninsula, gone on safari in Kenya's Masai Mara, and climbed to the roof of Notre-Dame Cathedral in Paris to stare in the face of the gargoyles. And, more importantly, I've become a writer. My writing has been published in *Essence* magazine; in the anthologies *Storming Heaven's Gate: An Anthology of Spiritual Writings by Women*, *The Public Library: A Photographic Essay*, and *Oakland Noir*; in a number of literary journals; and regularly in the *Oakland Heritage Alliance News*.

Acknowledgments

Writers often talk about how solitary a vocation writing is, but that claim is, at best, an exaggeration. This book couldn't have been written without the encouragement, editorial guidance, and friendship of a whole host of people. I am particularly indebted to the following: Elaine Kachavos, my high school creative writing teacher, generously broadened my understanding of writing's many gifts. Lydia Nayo was that other "other" in our San Francisco State creative writing class back in the day. She continues to inspire me with her sharp mind, devotion to the written word, and enduring friendship. Linda Burnham and Miriam Ching Louie, sister-friends and dedicated community organizers, listened to early drafts of this work during our "Craft Monday" sessions, and encouraged me to complete it when I thought no one would be interested in my story. My "beta" readers—friends Doug Smith, Susan Anderson, Carol Snow, Kate Kordich, and my beloved husband Gerald Chambers—provided careful readings and insightful comments of the manuscript that helped me a great deal. My instructors at

Acknowledgments

Goucher College's MFA Program in Creative Nonfiction—Lauren Slater and my thesis advisor, the late Philip Gerard—believed in my writing talent and encouraged me to push harder for deeper truths. The staff at the Hedgebrook writers' residency provided me with a nurturing environment to find my creative voice and, as a result, allowed me to imagine myself as a writer. A healthy dose of serendipity brought me and my memoir to Heyday's attention. I am indebted to publisher Steve Wasserman and his team at Heyday for their enthusiastic support of this work. They guided me through the publishing process with careful editorial attention and respect for my voice. Finally, and most importantly, I am endlessly indebted to my big sister Sarah Wright, who saved me by opening doors to the world of literature, loved me unconditionally, and said, "Yes, you can," in a thousand different ways. I give heartfelt thanks to all.

About the Author

DOROTHY LAZARD was born in St. Louis and grew up in San Francisco and Oakland. A librarian for nearly forty years, she joined the staff of the Oakland Public Library in 2000. From 2009 until her retirement in 2021, she was the head librarian of OPL's Oakland History Center, where she encouraged people of all ages and backgrounds to explore local history. She lives in Oakland.